May 2015

RENEWING THE FEAR
A Jew goes to Berlin

KeepAhead Monographs

1. Michael Selzer: *Snuffing Up The Wind. Theomonarchism in the Biblical Text* (2014)

2. Michael Selzer: *Renewing the Fear. A Jew goes to Berlin* (2014)

3. Michael Selzer: *The Symmetry Norm* (forthcoming, 2015)

4. Michael Selzer: *Politics and Human Perfectibility: A Jewish Perspective* (forthcoming, 2015)

Michael Selzer

RENEWING THE FEAR

A Jew goes to Berlin

*Ahi quanto a dir qual era è cosa dura ...
Che nel pensier rinova la paura.*

KeepAhead Monographs
Colorado Springs, CO
2014

First Edition

© Michael Selzer 2014. All Rights Reserved.

To the memory of
DANKWART RUSTOW
faithful friend

Table of Contents

Introduction	3
Day One	23
Day Two	37
Day Three	69
Day Four	89
Day Five	101
Day Six	123

Introduction[1]

I spent the first part of my childhood-the years from 1940 to 1946-among Germans. I spoke German. My playmates were German. I went to a German kindergarten, and it was there that I learned my alphabet, in German. I sang German songs. I still remember one of those songs. It begins, *Nun ade du mein lieb Heimatland, lieb Heimatland ade*: "Farewell now, my dear homeland, dear homeland, farewell".

Satara prison-camp school, 1944. I am third from the right in the front row.

Yet I was a Jew and not a German, and Germany was no homeland to me. In fact, I had no homeland or even a real home. From the time

---

[1] A version of this Introduction appeared previously in the *Journal of War, Literature and the Arts,* vol.26.

I was a few weeks old I had lived only in prison camps. These camps were in India. Our captors were the British, who then ruled India.

It was no secret in those days that the Jews had been excluded from German life and indeed were in the process of being excluded by the Germans from life itself. The policy of the German government was that a Jew cannot be a German (*der Jude kann nicht Deutscher sein*), and this was also a founding principle of law in the Third Reich. Few Germans challenged their Leader's assertion that almost every setback Germany ever experienced, and almost every danger it now faced, was caused by the Jews. Inspired by slogans such as *die Juden sind unser Unglück*-the Jews are our misfortune-the Germans were engaged in exterminating the entire Jewish people.

When World War 2 broke out the British government had to decide the fate of some fifty thousand German civilians, and a much smaller number of Jewish refugees from Germany, who were living in Britain and its overseas territories. Common sense dictated that the government's decision would be based on the obvious fundamental differences between the two groups. The Jewish refugees, after all, were the first victims of Nazi evil and had more reason than anyone to desire the defeat of Germany. The Germans on the other hand were Britain's enemies and were likely to do what they could to bring about Britain's defeat.

Incredibly, the British authorities decided to ignore the difference between the two groups and instead took the position that the Jewish refugees posed as great a potential threat to Britain's security as the Aryan Germans themselves. Accordingly, they issued orders that both groups-the Jews as well as the Germans-were to be rounded up forthwith and imprisoned. The captives were officially designated "enemy aliens" and "prisoners of war". The official euphemism was that they were "interned". The prisons in which they were held were sometimes called "internment camps", sometimes "prisoner of war camps", and sometimes "parole camps", because their inmates had given their word-"*parole*"-that they would not to try to escape. My parents, who had fled to India in 1938, were among those caught in the British dragnet. Not even the fact that my father had earlier been imprisoned by the Nazis could secure our freedom. And so it was that one morning in the late Fall of 1940, when I was about six weeks old, a squad of heavily-armed Indian policemen arrived at our house, handcuffed my parents, and under close guard brought us by train half-way across India to the prison camp on the outskirts of a little town in the Western Ghats called Purandhar.

At Purandhar my father was appointed the camp doctor. After some time he came to believe that the commandant of the camp was stealing the infirmary's medical supplies and selling them on the black market. He informed the Red Cross of this and they investigated the matter. I do not know what they found or what became of the commandant, but the result for us was that we were transferred to the far harsher camp in Satara. My earliest memories are set there. We lived in Nissen huts (the British forerunner of Quonset huts), without electricity or running water; even for children the long monsoon season was nightmarish. In later years I have met several people who also had been children in Satara. We all seem to have vivid memories of the place, but few that are pleasant.

A small number of our fellow-prisoners in Satara (but none of the other children) were Jews. The rest were Aryans, and most of them, as I understand, were Nazis or Nazi sympathizers. From time to time some would point to a tall tree in the camp and tell my parents and the other Jews: "This is where we'll hang you when Rommel comes to liberate us". Of course that was only until the autumn of 1942, when Hitler's dream of breaking through to India was buried forever in the sands of El Alamein. From then on almost all the Germans in the camp ceased ever having been followers of Hitler. Indeed, when the war was over some of them, including once-outspoken anti-Semites, went around asking Jews in the camp to sign documents certifying that they had always been anti-Nazis.

The end of the war did not at first change our circumstances. The British government was still officially blind to the difference between Aryans and Jews from Germany, and decided to "repatriate" them all to Germany: the Jews as well as the Aryans; the victims of Nazism as well as the Nazis themselves. This caused much distress to my parents and the other Jewish prisoners in the camp, who naturally enough did not think of Germany as their "Fatherland". I dimly remember once hearing that the Jews in our camp threatened to commit suicide *en masse* rather than let themselves be sent to Germany, but I don't know how accurate this recollection is.

Sometimes, indeed, I wonder how accurate *any* of my memories of Satara are. The facts seem too bizarre, too cruel, to be true.

In the summer of 1946 however the British rulers of India, who with the end of the Raj would soon be experiencing their own involuntary repatriation, changed their mind. They now allowed us to remain in India. We returned to Lahore, my birthplace, which the next year was absorbed into the new country of Pakistan.

In Lahore my German past quickly retreated into the shadows. I assumed (in every sense) a succession of new identities. Instead of German friends I now had Muslim ones; my German teachers were replaced, in turn, by Indian nuns (at the Convent of Jesus and Mary), Anglican clergymen (at the Cathedral School) and Belgian monks (at St. Anthony's School). I now spoke English-with a distinct Indian accent-and sang Christian hymns. Later, I went to Woodstock, a boarding school in India run by Protestant missionaries from the United States, where I sang patriotic American songs and acquired something like an American accent. After two years there I went to Bedales, a self-styled progressive school in England, and there I sang madrigals and acquired the more or less English accent that I still have.

These odd circumstances, and the discontinuities and fragments of which I think of myself as being in large measure composed, enriched my life and exposed me to an unusually wide range of languages, cultures, and ideologies. I was a poster child for what some people nowadays celebrate as "diversity" (and others, perhaps more wisely, deplore as *anomie*.)

On the other hand, having never encountered another human being whose circumstances resemble mine, I spent my childhood and adolescence without belonging to a community of people whose values and outlooks I could unconsciously absorb as my own, and be comfortable with-and whose mere presence would implicitly reassure me that it was acceptable to be whatever it was that I was becoming.

But what was that? What was I, and what was I becoming? I did not know how to answer these questions and by the time I was nine years old I already experienced that as an acute problem. Before leaving for boarding school in India, I asked my parents what I should tell people who wanted to know where I was from (I still dread being asked this question and still don't quite know how to answer it). The formula they suggested, "my parents are refugees from Germany, and I was born in the part of India that is now Pakistan", did little to reassure me. It was easier to know what I was not.

I was not much of a German, no matter what British officialdom had had to say on the matter. But I was *something* of one, as I will show presently.

I wasn't much of a Jew, either. My parents were unenthusiastic about their own Jewish identities and there was little that they said or did that helped me understand what it means to be a Jew or how to navigate my way through life as one. However, their attitude could not extinguish the longing I felt for some connection to the Jewish world; and whenever white people I didn't know came to our house in Lahore (I mistakenly assumed that all Jews were white) I would ask my parents, hopefully, whether they were Jews. But they never were. Other than my immediate family and the few Jewish families in the camps, I would be twelve years old before I so much as saw another Jew.

Nor could I identify myself as an Indian or (after 1947) as a Pakistani, for even a child could see that I wasn't one. In Lahore my parents arranged for me to take Urdu lessons once a week from the hunchbacked bookkeeper of the Gymkhana Club, but they were careful to do nothing else that might encourage me (heaven forbid!) to "go native"-that being in any case something that only my fellow-*Lahori* Kim, with his unique talents and guile, has ever been able to accomplish. That I was not Indian is also confirmed by a photograph taken in 1947 of me in a small group of children in a school play in Kashmir.

The Garden School, Kashmir, 1947.
I am second from the right in the front row.

What a telling image it is of a bygone world! Two of the children in the picture are Indian, and (appalling as it now seems) they are dressed as Kashmiri peasants. The boy, sitting somewhat apart from the group, has a bundle of firewood on his back; the girl is holding a basket filled with twigs on her head. The other six children are European and are dressed in fairy-tale garments. Those in the front row are holding sunflowers, those in the back have sprigs in their hands. Unlike the Indian children, who have sullen expressions, the Europeans are all smiling. I am sitting next to the Indian boy in the front row. I am wearing a silly costume, holding a flower and have a happy smile. Certifiably, therefore, I am not an Indian!

There was however one specific way in which the option of "going native" *was* available to me. Having been shorn of their German citizenship by the Nazis, my parents were officially "stateless" people. When they traveled abroad it was with a cumbersome document known as the Nansen passport that had been devised by the League of Nations for the use of refugees who no longer had travel papers issued by a sovereign state. Until 1947 I too was a stateless person and would have been eligible for the postwar equivalent of the Nansen passport. However, the fact that I had been born in the part of British India that became Pakistan meant that after India and Pakistan gained their independence in 1947 I was eligible for any one of three other passports: Indian, Pakistani, and British. My parents chose the latter for me, and so it was with a British passport that, at the age of nine, I traveled to the American boarding school in India.

But even this document was not without its peculiar ambiguities. My passport identified me simply as a "British subject", which was a temporary category that parliament in London had created for marginal characters from the colonies like me. A real English person would be identified additionally as a "citizen of the United Kingdom of Great Britain and Northern Ireland". Lacking that status, I was not entitled to vote in England, to run for public office or-after the Commonwealth Immigration Act was passed in 1962-even to live in England. So my nominal Englishness was in fact the kind that identified me as a somewhat Indian, Pakistani or other ambiguous person, and definitely not as English!

And this of course points to the fact that I was not English, either. Although I spent my entire adolescence and some of my early adulthood in England, I was never able to think of myself as English. To borrow a phrase: a Jew cannot be an Englishman, perhaps particularly not if he has spent the first five and a half years of his life imprisoned by His Majesty's Government as an enemy alien.

The barriers I encountered in England were social, psychological and intellectual. The social barriers were those of xenophobia and antisemitism, which at least in those days were both deeply ingrained in English life (a common saying of the time was that "Niggers begin in Calais"). The psychological barriers had to do with my unwillingness to mention Satara to anyone, and my inability to resolve the tension of living among and in many ways identifying with the people who had incarcerated my family and me there.[2]

The intellectual barrier was perhaps similar to that encountered by black Africans whose French colonial teachers made them refer to "Nos ancêtres les Gaulois"-our ancestors the Gauls. The matter came to a head for me when I was at Oxford. My subject there was history, which I loved, but the curriculum was almost entirely in English history, and I began to suspect that as long as I studied English history I would never possess the intuitive sympathy with my subject, or at least the intuitive insight into it, that any good historian must have. After my return to Oxford from Jerusalem, where I had covered the trial of Adolf Eichmann, I felt that I must not delay my decision any longer, and that I must now study Jewish, and not English, subjects. Only in this way, I reasoned,

---

[2] I recently came across a letter that the headmaster of Bedales wrote to my mother when I was fifteen. With remarkable insight, he told her that I suffered from "a feeling of being 'different', in particular of having no firm roots here, in the shape of either a home in this country or British nationality. The last is very evident."

would I be able to experience the closeness to my past – in my case, perhaps an illusory notion! - that the study of English history would always deny me. My decision was not supported by my tutors. R. W. Southern, the great medievalist and someone I esteemed highly for his personal qualities as well as for his scholarship, reacted to it with considerable annoyance and never spoke to me again. My other tutor, Christopher Hill, who was not without his own curious ambiguities, responded only with polite disdain. Undeterred, I bade farewell to my *soi-disant* ancestors the Gauls and set about familiarizing myself with the Semitic languages and literature of my true ancestors.

Thankfully, most of the issues that arose out of my strange circumstances eventually resolved themselves. I grew out of some, discovered how to compensate for many, and left others behind me when I came to the United States and found it remarkably easy and attractive to start thinking of myself as an American and an American Jew.

But my German problem, the earliest challenge to my efforts to recognize myself, still persists. I don't imagine that I will ever overcome it.

In the camps I naturally assumed that I was German, just like all my friends. But I knew from my parents that we wanted the British to win the war-they were the good side-and for the Germans, who were bad, to lose it. This however raised some questions in my mind that did nothing but baffle me. If the British were good, I wanted to know, why had they imprisoned us? Was it because *we* were bad? That didn't seem likely. And what about everyone else in the camp-my friends, and all the grownups whom we called *Onkel* or *Tante*-uncle and aunt? With the exception of *die alte Hexe*-the old witch-a mean old woman who frightened all the children in the camp, it was unimaginable to me that these "uncles" and "aunts" of ours were bad people. I knew them only as ordinary and likable folk-some of them were the parents of my friends-and they never showed me any hostility that I was aware of (though I now recognize that at least some of them must have regarded me with the same murderous hatred that they felt for all Jews).

One day, however, my mother told me that I must stop calling these people *Onkel* or *Tante*. "I won't have you calling Nazis 'uncle' or 'aunt'", she said, and instructed me from then on to address them instead as *Herr* or *Frau*-Mr. or Mrs. I can still remember the awkwardness I felt when I spoke to an erstwhile *Onkel* or *Tante* in this new way for the first time. I don't recall any of them reacting to it, or any of my friends asking me about it, but I'm sure the change must have been noticed and commented on.

Strange as it may now seem, I do not believe that I had any inkling of what the word "Nazi" really meant. I could tell of course that it applied to the Germans around me, but that did not lead me to regard them as significantly different from me and my parents, and it did not challenge my sense of being somehow connected to all of them. They were after all the parents of my playmates and-with the exception of the few Jews (all of whom were childless) in the camp-they were the only adults I knew.[3]

In the years after the war the problem of my *German-ness* (for want of a better term) became more pressing. Often this was because of the example set by my parents. In Satara they had not wanted me to call Germans *Onkel* or *Tante*, but it did not take them very long, once we were freed from the camp, to fashion an altogether different reality for themselves. They now spent part of their foreign vacation every other year in Germany. They bought German cars and German medical equipment. My father brought a physician from Germany to assist him in his practice (it was only later that this man emerged in his true colors as a virulent anti-

---

[3] Among my playmates were the two children of a Lutheran minister who lived in the same Nissen hut as we. Only a thin partition separated our quarters, and twice a day my parents would have to hear this man saying, as part of grace over the family meal, beseeching God to grant victory to Germany and to bless the Fuehrer.

Semite and a veteran of the Waffen-SS). My father also did nothing to discourage people from referring to him as "the Germany doctor", an honorific (as it was intended to be) that proved useful to his practice since the hostility Indians and Pakistanis in those years felt toward the British often led them to favor German physicians. In his later years my father became a fast friend of the German ambassador to Pakistan (whom, as far as I know, he never asked about his activities during the Hitler years), and he agreed to be the honorary German consul-general in Lahore. My mother however vetoed the idea; as she told my father, she could not live in a house which had a German flag flying over it. As consolation prize my father was offered, and with my mother's assent accepted, the *Bundesverdienstkreuz,* a German decoration for his services (whatever they may have been) to the Federal Republic. By then, my parents had both become German citizens. Rather curiously, my father found ways to merge his hostility to me (the reason for which remain a mystery) with his inclination toward the Germans. It seemed to give him pleasure to tell me that he regretted sending me to boarding school in England rather than Germany where, or so he claimed, educational standards were much higher; and when I was at Oxford he would try to convince me of its inferiority to the great German universities (none of which he had attended).

The irony of this never escaped me. For my father was not in fact a German Jew. He was born in Galicia, then a province of the Austro-Hungarian empire and now part of the Ukraine, from where his family moved to Germany shortly before the outbreak of World War I. Snubbed by real German Jews (including by members of my mother's family) as a mere *Galitsianer,* my father felt his inferior status very acutely. What balm it was to his wounded pride therefore that now, as a distinguished physician, he was honored by the German government and could allow himself to feel accepted as an equal by Germans of high status. His apotheosis culminated when, during a hike in the Bavarian mountains, his friend the German ambassador to Pakistan proposed that they henceforth address each other with the intimate *Du* instead of with the formal *Sie* they had used previously.

My father was the first exemplar I ever encountered of the very sorry process in which a socially-inferior person rejects his own background and attempts to remodel himself in the image of those who disdain him. Later I would understand how widespread this phenomenon is. It characterized much of the encounter of Indians (among them men and women of great refinement) with their British overlords (among them men and women lacking every sort of refinement). It was also a troubling leitmotif of nineteenth- and twentieth-century Jewish history, marking much of the encounter of East European Jews, in particular, with the West, and then, after the establishment of the state of Israel in 1948, with their own Jewish brethren from the Muslim world. I explored this theme in some detail in my first book and was widely rebuked at the time. Nearly 50 years later it is being taken seriously by some Israeli scholars.

I regarded my parents' attitudes toward Germany as shameful, and on more than one occasion I all too tactlessly told them so. In some dark moments I even wondered whether the ambiguities that their enthusiastic accommodation to the "new" Germany exposed may have been what led the British to keep us imprisoned for so long. (Many Jews, and even some Aryans, were released from the camps a few months after being arrested.)

I cannot pretend however to be entirely free of the sentiments that drew my parents back to their German roots. Although Satara was a very long time ago some of the German strands that were woven into my being there remain part of me. I find that I welcome the opportunity to speak German. There are German words and phrases that have a particular resonance for me that I cannot discover in any other language. At school and university I opted for German as my modern foreign language, instead of French, and I found, much to my astonishment, that I speak French with a German accent. I was told this by a taxi driver in Ghent who was adamant that there was no cathedral in his town (I had come from Brussels to see Van Eyck's *Adoration of the Mystic Lamb*) but who suddenly remembered where it was after I produced my passport to show him that no, despite what he thought he heard, I am not a German. Just a few years ago, driving along a valley near our house, I meant to say to my companion, "This is such a wide valley", but what I said was, "This is such a *breit* valley"-"*breit*" being the German word for "wide". We now refer to it as "the bright valley"! Although I won't listen to Wagner, I find vocal or choral music far more engaging when it is sung in German than in any other tongue. For many years there was no form of music I enjoyed more than nineteenth-century German *Lieder*, or art songs, to which I had been introduced by my mother. When I meet Germans it sometimes seems to me, at first, as though an unspoken bond connects us, a mutual recognition that only we could share; and I need to remind myself that there is no such bond, and that my "recognition" is unilateral, unreciprocated, chimerical: altogether delusional; and I then feel as though I have been guilty of profound absurdity and disloyalty.

My German-ness, therefore, only went so far. If anything, the example set by my parents pushed me in the opposite direction. Certainly, it did nothing to moderate the perception that began growing in me from the time I was just 12 or 13 that the only fact about the Germans that matters to me is that they murdered six million Jews and would have murdered the rest of us if they had been able to do so. Absolute and uncompromising rejection of any connection at all with Germany and its people became, in my view, the only course for a Jew who wants to retain his integrity and self-respect and be faithful to the memory of all those millions - *all those millions* - whom the Germans murdered.

This attitude expresses itself in a variety of ways, which I set down here without feeling any need to justify or explain them.

For all my pleasure in the German language I bristle when I hear people speaking it. I make a definite point of not buying things manufactured in Germany and I do not drink German wine or beer. Even in the most careless days of my youth I would never go out with a German woman, for it seemed to me that younger Germans differed only in degree, and not in kind, from their parents and grandparents. When I learned of the Morgenthau Plan for the "pastoralization" of Germany - it called for the dismantling of German factories, the flooding of mines and other steps aimed at sending Germany back to its relatively harmless rural past - I was sorry that there were practical reasons why it could not be implemented. I was appalled by the cynicism that led the Germans to call their program of restitution and compensation payments to Jews *Wiedergutmachung* - that is to say, "Making good again".

I started to feel that I must ensure that the Holocaust will always remain a presence in my life, familiarizing myself with it as historical fact and immersing my imagination in its horrors. As the correspondent of an Oxford undergraduate magazine I attended the first few weeks of the Eichmann trial in Jerusalem. At the trial I learned that the Allies had rebuffed the pleas of Jewish leaders to bomb the railroad tracks leading to Auschwitz. On my return to England I pestered every politician I encountered, including on one occasion prime minister Harold Macmillan, with demands for an explanation. (The replies I received were always evasive. "I want to assure you", Macmillan told me, "that one of the reasons we wanted to win the war was to put an end to the extermination of the Jews".) Years later I interviewed Albert Speer, one of the major Nazi war criminals, after he was released from Spandau. I also interviewed Hitler's evil image maker, Leni Riefenstahl. I co-authored a book analyzing the Rorschach responses of the major Nazi war criminals (among them, Speer) who were put on trial in Nuremberg. I assembled a valuable archive of psychological test responses of other Nazis, including Adolf Eichmann, that I deposited in the Library of Congress. It was an obsession with me to discredit Hannah Arendt's notion that the Nazis were merely spineless ordinary people - she called them "banal" - who obeyed orders. I wrote a book about the day on which Dachau was liberated by American troops. I tried, though without success, to get the German government or German foundations to make a comprehensive inventory of all sites of Jewish significance in Germany, and to place historical markers on the more important ones. One of my more bizarre ideas was to have my forearm tattooed with the concentration camp number of a murdered Jew - no doubt, it is just as well that I did not follow through with that...

The idea of having a tattoo was inspired by the feeling that something of great importance was missing from my attitude toward Germany and the Germans. Whenever I thought about the Holocaust I did so, as it were, in the third person: it was something that happened to other people. I was connected to them in a very real sense, of course, but it was as an observer who is connected to the thing observed - connected, to be sure, by intense sympathy and detailed knowledge, but always from a distance and not at all as part of their world. The immense sorrow I felt for the victims did not make their pain mine. The catastrophe had befallen *them* and not me.

In a certain respect of course this distancing of myself from them made sense. Satara was no Auschwitz. Six million were dead but I was alive. Compared to what they had suffered my victimhood (if indeed it could be called that) was trivial.

Yet wasn't it true that Satara and Auschwitz *were* linked, even if only as different ends of the same continuum? Could I grasp the horrors of the Holocaust if I did not approach them through the gateway of my own experience? And could I, for that matter, adequately comprehend my own experience if I failed to acknowledge the far more terrible circumstances with which it was distantly but nevertheless integrally associated?

For years these questions lurked, seldom acknowledged and never really addressed, in the deep background of my mind. My parents, I now recognize, had always been reluctant to talk about Satara, and even though they would usually answer my questions about it, my questions themselves were haphazard and never really touched on the important issues. As a family we put Satara behind us, ignored it. It was not one of the reference points of our lives, although we often talked about the Holocaust itself. In England, as I have already mentioned, I continued this pattern of avoidance. Quite recently I had lunch with John Slater, who had been one of my favorite teachers at Bedales. For a reason I no longer remember I mentioned our imprisonment in Satara. John was startled, and then became very agitated. "Why didn't anyone tell us about that?", he wanted to know: "Why not your parents, why not you?" "But why should we have?", I asked. "What difference would it have made?". "Oh", replied John, " it would have made a very big difference indeed". He was right, of course, but I changed the subject. It was still not something I cared to discuss.

There were episodic, limited, exceptions. The Holocaust became very personal for me with the birth of each of my children. Holding the newborn Sarah, Abigail, Adam in my arms for the first time I could not help thinking that it was children like these - a *million* or so of them - whom the Nazis murdered. With great force but only fleetingly this thought placed me directly in the setting of horror that I had always avoided.

As time went by I also came to see myself as part of the generation of those million murdered children and I started to recognize how decisively and comprehensively our existence was constricted by their absence:

> *We are the diminished generation*
> *Brittled gleaning of hate-harvested fields:*

> *A generation that almost wasn't*
> *And therefore isn't quite,*
> *A lonely generation,*
> *Only few in number,*
> *And never quite of where we are;*
> *Inept with nuances,*
> *Articulating what others needn't:*
> *Audience of someone else's play.*
> *A generation that must dissemble,*
> *Pretending that we too belong*
> *To the natural flow of things...*

Of course, we Jews have always been "a people that dwells apart and is not counted among the nations" (*Numbers* 23:9). But my generation is a minority among this minority.

Many of those million murdered children would have grown up to be people of vision and learning, repositories of Israel's profound values. Without them our generation is depleted, not only in numbers but spiritually, a hedonistic and ambitious generation that is easily beguiled by slogans and programs and cannot rise to the challenges with which history confronts us in the aftermath of the Holocaust. We leave a cruelly-impoverished legacy to our children, and I fear that they will impoverish it still further.

The recognition of myself as part of this diminished generation brought me from a third-person encounter with the Holocaust to one in the first-person plural. The tragedy had not befallen *them* alone, it had also befallen my generation – *us* – too. My ability to recognize this was progress, but only to a sort of half-way point at best. For *"they"* and *"we"* do not encompass the entirety of the Holocaust or any other chapter of our history. The "I" is contained in them and alone gives them full validity. In the drama of the Exodus from Egypt – as we are told (Exodus 13.8) and read every year in the Passover *seder* – "The Lord acted for *me*, when *I* came out of Egypt".

Nevertheless, for many years the "We" was as far as I could take my equation. The "I" remained stubbornly outside it. One day however, and for no apparent reason, the thought came to me that I ought to spend some time in Germany: specifically, in Berlin. At first the idea made no sense to me at all. The prospect of being in Berlin, *annus mundi,* the very center of the Third Reich, surrounded by Germans, was not just senseless but chilling and repulsive.

Yet the thought would not leave me. I started to feel as though it were a summons that I must obey. And it was now that, again for no apparent reason, I began to meditate on the words of Deuteronomy 25:17. I repeated them to myself over and over again as if I were a hippy embracing his mantra. I had used those words as the motto of a book I had written with Florence Miale a quarter of a century earlier. It was only now, however, that I saw that the injunction was not to "remember what Amalek *did* " but - *specifically!* - to remember what Amalek "did to *you*". The pronoun is *lecha,* that is, the second person singular. "Remember what Amalek did to you"!

This simple exegesis had an extraordinary impact on me. It showed me that it was not enough for me to remember what the Germans had done to the Jews as such, or even what they had done to my generation of Jews. I was commanded to remember, to be aware of, to expose myself to, *what they had done to me.*

It was also clear to me that the *"lecha* – to you" was somehow linked to the summons, as I thought of it, go to Berlin. My sorrow over all those deaths, all that destruction, my awareness of the sad predicament of my generation's feebleness, would remain incomplete until I forged the link that had been missing. I now understood that Satara was the context in which *I* had lived through the Holocaust: that it was *my* connection to the incomparably greater tragedy. Remarkably, this recognition was soon followed a series of dreams about Satara, the first I think I ever had. I will not describe those dreams, though I think I will remember them all my life, for their images of murderous evil and the sense of doom they conveyed are too appalling. But I valued them nevertheless. They were my dreams, my gateways into the terrain that I now needed to explore. And they too seemed to confirm that I must go to Berlin.

Day One

Boston: I noticed quite an Arab presence here at Logan Airport. One of the INS (I suppose now Department of Homeland Security) people inspecting passports is a Muslim woman whose entire person, other than her face and hands, are covered in a blue *hijab* and gown. Not surprisingly, everyone passing through this point avoids her, choosing instead to show their passports to one of the more "our kind" of security people, even though this means a longish wait. I would love to know what idiot in our federal bureaucracy thought that America's security is strengthened by placing in this strategic spot an official who looks like the handmaiden of a Saudi princeling.

And behind the Bon Pain counter in the departure lounge is a staff of three surly North African Arab women, who seem to have at most a few words of English between them. Boston, evidently, is back to being the warm and cuddly home of political correctitude. The stern common sense that prevailed in the immediate aftermath of 9/11 has almost disappeared. How many times will we have to go through this lamentable cycle before we steel ourselves to be and do what we must in face of Islam's assaults?

The last time I flew from here was in late September, 2001, just days after the attacks. We were going to Ireland to see Adam, and to England for Lilly's 90th birthday - commitments we wanted to keep. The departure lounge then was dim and gloomy, and none of the shops and restaurants that flank it was open. It was also chillingly quiet. Armed men from many different services – local and state police, national guardsmen, US deputy marshals, FBI agents – were everywhere, moving in small groups, some of them with police dogs. Suddenly, the world had become unfamiliar and disconcerting. Yet the ordinariness of things still retained a presence, and it was difficult to believe – I mean to believe *completely* – that it was from here that the catastrophic attacks had been launched.

Looking up from my newspaper I saw three young Arab men. They wore poorly-made suits and had a several days' growth of beard on their faces. They didn't look all that different from Mohammad Atta and his henchmen who, just a fortnight earlier, had also flown out of this very airport. I wondered how the ones I was now seeing could have passed through the security checks we had just cleared. Was it possible that security at Logan had once again failed? Were we going to be on the same flight as these men?

My wife hadn't noticed them. I stood up and told her I was going to stretch my legs for a few moments. I caught up with the three men and, passing them, heard that yes, they were indeed speaking Arabic – Egyptian Arabic, I thought. In moments like these it seems impossible to imagine that people who in every way appear to be human beings more or less just like anyone else might really be hell-bent on carrying out the most terrible, inhumane, deeds. I hesitated at first. Wasn't I being bigoted? Surely I wouldn't let myself think that all young Arab men are terrorists? Yet wasn't it better to be safe than politically correct? It wasn't much of a debate: I stopped a state trooper and asked him if he'd noticed the three Arabs. I nodded in their direction. He said, "Holy shit! No, I didn't see them before. I'll get back to you." I told him where I was sitting. After a while I saw him in a huddle with a U.S. marshal and a couple of FBI agents. One of them was talking on his two-way radio. A little while later the trooper found me and said that the Arabs had been thoroughly screened and searched and that, as he put it, "they're probably OK". I asked if he knew where they were flying. "Not the Aer Lingus to Dublin, I hope!" I said. "No", he replied. "They're taking the Lufthansa flight to Frankfurt."

That was four years ago, almost to the day. The two flights are still at adjoining gates. The Aer Lingus plane is just moving out. In about ten minutes I'll be getting on the Lufthansa flight to Frankfurt. I'm reminded once again that the past is not a foreign land.

No more than fifteen years ago a memo was circulated among the staff of the official government German National Tourist Office in New York instructing them to actively discourage Jews, Hispanics and Blacks from going to Germany. We know this because someone sent a copy of the memo to *The New York Times*, which published it. Talk of a smoking gun! I look at the other passengers waiting at the Lufthansa gate. I seem to be the only Jew here, and as far as I can tell there are no Blacks or Hispanics among us. Word gets out, I suppose, even if no longer through the German National Tourist Office. This doesn't seem particularly surprising to me. I remember Reggie telling me that he spent some time in Munich on an art scholarship that Hans Morgenthau had arranged for him after he saw Reggie's paintings in a street fair in Chicago. Reggie felt so uncomfortable in Germany, as a Black person, that he left after a month or two.

(Like my father, Morgenthau accepted the Federal Cross of Merit - *Bundesverdienstkreuz* - decoration from the German government. I don't get it!)

I mull over two conversations I had yesterday. Andy Sullivan came by in the morning, and startled me by saying that he hoped I would be able to find some forgiveness for the Germans on my trip.

"Why?" I replied. "It's not up to me to forgive Germans".

"But isn't it always good to forgive?"

"With the Germans it's better to remember, and remembering what they did to us makes it impossible to forgive them."

"But wouldn't you feel better if you stopped hating them?"

"Why should I feel better?" I asked him.

I wonder now whether there wasn't just a hint of posturing, of melodrama perhaps, of "please feel sorry for me", in my remarks – especially the "why should I feel better?" But what *does* one say about all this to someone who is not a Jew? Or to a Jew, for that matter? I really do not know how one rises to the enormity, the solemnity, of this subject. When German officials try to do so I think they're being hypocrites or else are enjoying a fleeting moment of self-aggrandizing masochism – Albert Speer's "I'm the most guilty person in the world" - before returning to their more-accustomed postures. (I also think that Germans are particularly eloquent on the subject when they speak to a Jewish audience, which I suspect they do far more frequently than to an Aryan one.) And when the Israelis speak about it I frequently think they are exploiting it for their political advantage (but then, why shouldn't they?!) I don't know who has found an appropriate voice. Not Elie Wiesel, to be sure: I think of him as the Holocaust's Glen Campbell. Perhaps Nellie Sachs' poems come close; and also Yevtushenko, my not-entirely-philosemitic friend Genya, who does so well in "Babi Yar", I think, with his outrage and compassion drawing you into all those place and all those times.

All those places! All those times!

Andy had wanted to know why I was going to Germany, and I told him that I really wasn't sure, but that that was something I seemed to feel I needed to do. It occurs to me just now that part of the reason may have to do with my age. I'm becoming old. In a few weeks I will be 65. I feel that I still have the emotional and physical energy for this undertaking, but that I won't necessarily have it in a few years' time. Besides, I want to be in Germany before the last of that generation has died out. I gather that about 6 million (that figure!) Germans who were born before 1930 are still alive. I want to look at them in their native habitat.

The other conversation I am thinking about now took place at dinner last night at the Goldberg's, with a woman called Edith, who

– though I don't think I've seen her before – has for years had an antique shop just down the road in Sheffield. From her accent it was obvious that she is a German. Things got off to an interesting start when, after Jean-Claude told her that I was going to Berlin, she asked: "Are you German?"

I think a person has to be particularly crass to ask me that question and I responded, in German, *der Jude kann nicht Deutscher sein*, a Jew cannot be a German. To which Edith replied, in tones of beatific innocence, "Oh, why do you say that?"

It was clear that we were not going to be friends, but I thought that I owed it to Jean-Claude and Lilly to be polite to the woman. Presently, she asked me if it was fair of me to associate all Germans with what happened in the Holocaust. "When I meet a German person", I replied, "I try to see him – or her – both as a human being and, that is to say additionally, as a German."

"Oh I hear that all the time", Edith responded (not altogether plausibly, I thought), "and you have no idea how much I suffer from it, etc., etc." But my probing – what exactly, or even approximately, does she find so upsetting about that? Didn't she too see herself as both a human being and as a German, among many other attributes; and didn't she see me as both a man and as a Jew? – elicited no more than some aspersions, no doubt fully justified, about my character; and further statements to the effect that were it not for her affection for Jean-Claude and Lilly she would already have left the party; that one of her best friends is a Jew who had published a book about his experiences during the war ("I can't bear to read about how he suffered"); and that her ex-husband is a Jew (his parents had boycotted the wedding because she is a German).

By now, Jean-Claude and Lilly both had their antennae out and, a little prematurely, called us to the table. While we were waiting for Lilly to bring the first course Jean-Claude asked Edith (he *is* a trouble-maker!) where in Germany she was from. And this is what she said:

> I was born in Essen, before the war. By 1943 the Allied bombing had become so bad that my mother couldn't take it any longer – she had two small children and one on the way – and so she moved us to Berchtesgaden, where we joined my father, who was stationed there.

No one said anything, but Edith looked perfectly relaxed, as though there was nothing notable about the fact that her father was stationed in the small town where Hitler had his vacation home, as did Goering, Speer, Bormann and other leading Nazis. Without doubt, all military personnel in Berchtesgaden – like her father - were there to guard Hitler, and it is equally certain that every last man and woman among them had been carefully screened for racial and ideological purity. Edith's antecedents were becoming much clearer to me.

"Tell us about Berchtesgaden", I said.

"It's a beautiful spot in the Bavarian Alps. My sisters and I love it so much that we are thinking of buying a small vacation house there!"

"And what else about it?" I asked.

"Nothing", she replied. "It's just a beautiful spot in the Bavarian Alps".

Here are some items that I found by Googling Berchtesgaden:

Hitler's house in Berchtesgaden is now an inn, which is described on its website in the following words:

> Board a breathtaking bus journey up the Kehlstein road and a luxurious brass elevator up through the rock into Kehlsteinhaus, known in English as the Eagle's Nest. Enjoy its impressive views and its excellent cuisine. The site combines a unique example of historic architecture and a stunning alpine setting.

The inn has a shop that sells a book about Hitler's connection to the place, and also a baseball cap with "Kehlsteinhaus Berchtesgaden" embroidered on it. That would be quite some souvenir to bring home! But imagine (I can't) enjoying "excellent cuisine" in Hitler's former country house, while pondering the "historic" nature of its architecture.

I went to the town's website, and enjoyed this description of its museum:

> *Everything that had once validity in Berchtesgaden, is exposed in the local heritage museum in the palace "Adelsheim", a representative building of the late Renaissance. Many exhibits remind of the former "Augustiner Chorherrenstift" of Berchtesgaden, likewise of the "Bavarian king house", of the middle society, of earlier rural life and of historical clothings. Finally in the palace "Adelsheim" also a sales room of the Berchtesgadener handicraft art is accommodated . This manifold and oft-quoted people art could be received in many branches.*

Evidently, Hitler and his gang are not among "everything that had once validity in Berchtesgaden" - they are no longer part of the "local heritage". (I've noticed that even educated Germans lapse into incredibly poor English when certain matters of their local heritage are being discussed or, rather, being *not* discussed.)

I just remembered now that in my Dachau book I mention a beautifully hand-carved and polychromed sign that stood atop a decorative pole in the parking lot of the concentration camp. The words on it were something to this effect: "Welcome to Dachau, the famous center of medieval German art".

Oh that local heritage! I wonder whether there is any place in this evil land without it.

Just now too I remember something Kitty once told me about a professional conference she attended in Munich a few years ago. At one session the German chairman announced that at the end of the day's deliberations he would be taking everyone to dinner at the nearby town of Dachau. This led one of the participants, an Englishman, to raise his hand and ask, as if thinking out aloud, "Dachau? Dachau? The name sounds familiar, but I can't place it. What's Dachau known for?" Quick as a wink their host responded, "Dachau – it's a beautiful old town that was a famous art center in the middle ages".

On which subject (or more or less on it) I recall that many, many years ago when I was still at Oxford I wrote a review of a German book about monuments to the Holocaust in what was then the Federal Republic of Germany. One of these structures was inscribed simply with the motto, *Der Mensch Sei Mensch!* - "humans are humans", which seemed to me to sidestep wonderfully the real issue while at the same time placing the murderers on the same level as their victims: as if it were just by chance that the Germans murdered six million Jews rather than the other way around. Another monument referred to the "Germans of the Jewish faith" of that particular town "who were taken away and died". Still another condemned anti-Semitism as "a lack of self-discipline", the implication being (or so I assume) that although the Jews are really awful one should have enough self-control not to acknowledge that one thinks so.

The Germans like to decontaminate their toxic sites, especially those which are in "beautiful spots" such as the Bavarian Alps. The sad truth is that the Germans' zeal for this task is not unbounded; and what they seem to overlook is that if a site isn't properly cleaned up the toxins will embed themselves more deeply than ever in the soil – and in the soul.

* * * *

The flight was called. I was grateful for a seat on the aisle. Next to me was a German man of about my age, but in far better physical condition. He had stood out in the crowd of people waiting to check in at the Lufthansa desk. Bronzed and muscular, he carried an enormous backpack with apparent ease, but what particularly struck me about him was his pate, which was the shiniest I think I have ever seen.

I've crossed the Atlantic for business, for research, to lecture, to see friends and children, and also just for the pleasure of traveling, but I've never gone on a trip like this one, clouded as it is by so much uncertainty and anxiety – fear even – all of which are no less intense for being so amorphous. I imagine that this is more or less what I would feel like if I were traveling to a hospital for an operation or to a courthouse to defend myself against a lawsuit – perhaps even if I was going off to fight in a war. I have no anticipation of encountering anything that will be of great interest to me, or give me pleasure. I am traveling voluntarily for a purpose I can't identify, to a place I detest, and for an encounter that I dread – even though I don't really know what that encounter will be with, or for that matter whether it will really occur. I've no reason to suppose I'll be any the wiser or better for subjecting myself to all this.

Che strano!

I put my own, puny, backpack (my only piece of luggage: it contains enough changes of clothing for the week, my toilet things, a small camera, and a copy of Goldhagen's *Hitler's Willing Executioners* that Lilly had lent me) in the overhead compartment. Much to my embarrassment, it fell down onto the lap of my neighbor. Naturally, I apologized – in English – but he continued to stare straight ahead, as though he had noticed neither me nor my backpack. Oh dear!

The doors slammed shut, the light dimmed, there was a hiss of air – and then the usual preliminaries about safety procedures, meals, and so on. They were delivered in German and then in fluent English, but not in French or any other continental language.

I realized that I was now at the point of no return. Until I actually boarded the plane I was not completely certain that I would actually do so. Now I feel acutely anxious – though about nothing I can specify – and my reflexive hostility to Germans asserts itself as an actual, physical, tremor in my stomach. I am absolutely certain that everyone knows I am a Jew, and that this knowledge does not bring them much by way of pleasure. I feel my anger rising, and my anxiety. I had intended to start reading the Goldhagen book once I was seated, or at least have it on my lap, but I now don't dare to! I am also apprehensive about having ordered a kosher meal. Why? Do I expect to be attacked by my fellow passengers for these irrefutable evidences of my despicable origins? I know I am being paranoid, but I don't try to talk myself out of it. It feels like an apt frame of mind, under the circumstances. I begin to hyperventilate…

I still don't have an idea of why I'm going to Germany, only that I felt, all of a sudden (was it really only ten days ago?), that I needed to do so, and that perhaps there are things for me to attend to there, matters that must be faced, a past to engage with, though with no expectation of victory or defeat (or even what they might look like). But at the moment I don't believe the trip will resolve anything at all for me. A coven of working-class Catholic women from Medford are among my fellow-travelers on this flight. They are pilgrims – gullible, excited, confident. They have their opiate and know why they are going, and they seem incapable of doubting that they will find what they are looking for. In the departure lounge I overheard one of them say something like this: "I knew that if I fell on my knees and prayed real hard just as she was dying she would take my message straight to Jesus". It seems very strange to me that any adult in an advanced society of the twenty-first century could believe such nonsense! For me there is no Jesus, of any kind. Indeed, there is no message. But I did order a kosher meal for the flight, even though I'm not a kosher kind of Jew, because it seemed to me that making myself known as a Jew would be an appropriate gesture of defiance. Why though do I want to make myself known as a Jew. To whom? And to what end? And why in a spirit of defiance? I feel a little embarrassed by myself. I hope that this self that I am advertising is more authentic and less exhibitionistic than is implied by my ordering a kosher meal. I will feel deflated if every German, seeing this kosher-eating Jew, will make nice to me. That, I can say with confidence, would pose a big obstacle to whatever it is that I am up to on this trip. But I shouldn't worry. It's always easy to stop people being nice! But I fear that the Germans' swinishness, for now only sub-coetaneous, will be roused by my presence, and that I will crumble at my very first encounter with it. Yet I also I want to look into the German cloaca and see myself reflected in its disgusting mire. Fanya Fenelon mentions, in *Playing for Time*, that women at Auschwitz had to sit on the concrete rim of a huge open tank when they relieved themselves. That scene defies imagination, but she goes on to say that she once saw a woman, sick (as so many were) with dysentery and too weak to support herself, fall into the tank and drown in the excrement. Why would I want to look into that? But then, why did that woman die, why was there an Auschwitz, why the Nazis? One can't really live, it seems to me, without knowing with horrible vividness that those things did happen and accepting that there is no grand reason *sub specie aeternitatis* for them. But is it anything more than luck and perhaps self-control that saves one from falling into that pit? And what is this "see myself reflected in its disgusting mire" all about. Possibly, something to do with my own cloaca?

What am I doing to myself?

I feel some presentiment, a foreboding of – something. But these are commonplace for me. It is only since I decided to go on this trip that they have cast themselves into a specifically German setting.

But no. That's untrue. A part of my life has been lived in that setting since at least the time I attended the Eichmann trial in Jerusalem in 1961. How often have I seen myself in the cattle cars, at the entrance to the gas chambers, at the moment when one's hiding place is betrayed by a neighbor, at the moment, too, when one thinks of fighting back but is too terrified or resigned to do so: and in all those other tormented moments... And my Nazi dreams. Oh god, my Nazi dreams! Those also go back a long time. I don't want to describe them – they are too appalling – except to say that some of them are set in towns with old, soot-covered stone buildings three or four stories high flanking streets or squares paved with cobblestones. It seems remarkable to me how detailed the architectural elements of these dreams are. And it occurs to me now that I might stumble upon some of these very street scenes from my dreams when I am in Berlin! Wouldn't that be something? Is that why I have felt this call to go to Berlin? It also occurs to me now that in the Nazi dreams set in Germany I am essentially a passive observer of danger and brutality, while in the dreams set in the camps - actually, I only remember dreams set in Satara, the last of the camps we were in - I commit acts of appalling violence, and even murder. I shall certainly disregard any inner call that might come for me to go to Satara!

By my count this is my eighth trip to Germany. I'm astonished to realize that I've been to Germany more often than to any other country on the Continent. My first trip was way back in 1954, during the summer holidays, when I was 13. My mother and I visited Cologne and Düsseldorf, and then Oberhausen, an awful, impoverished industrial town in the Ruhr where we found the grim little smoke-stained house in which my father grew up. In all these cities we saw bombed-out buildings, and others whose walls were pitted with bullet holes. I distinctly remember how much satisfaction it gave me to see this destruction, though I think that stemmed more from my identification with the British (I was at school in England) than with the Jews. We ended the trip on a steamer traveling down the Rhine from Mainz to Coblenz, a voyage that took us between hills terraced with vineyards and capped by ruined castles. Our fellow passengers drank wine or beer as they watched the scenery unfold, and sang sentimental German songs with great fervor. I joined in singing the ones I knew. One of these was *O du wunderschöner deutscher Rhein* ("oh you wonderfully beautiful German Rhine". I don't believe there's any other place in the world where people celebrate a river as belonging to their country.) Naturally, when we cruised past the Lorelei we all sang *Ich weiß nicht, was soll es bedeuten...* ("I don't know what it means that I'm so sad").

The Nazis banned the Lorelei song because it was written by the Jew, Heine. It was so popular however, so rooted in the German soul, that people nevertheless went on singing it throughout "those years". This is presumably one of the very few – or perhaps the only – instance of large numbers of Germans refusing to go along with the Nazis' hatred of everything (and no matter how tenuously) Jewish. And the question worth pondering is that if the Nazis backed down on this point, as they did, what else would they have stopped doing if only enough Germans had spoken up for decency? Well, there's another instance, of course. Among the Nazis' earliest initiatives, once they gained power, was their so-called "euthanasia" program, that led them to gas tens of thousands of mentally retarded people. The popular outcry against this program was so loud and sustained that the Nazis felt obliged to end it. Of course, there was no outcry at all against the Nazis' program of exterminating the Jewish people. There is at least a possibility that the Nazis would have ended that program, too, if there had been any real public opposition to it. Remembering this only increases my recognition of the culpability of all Germans. Their outcry could have saved six million Jews. But they chose instead to keep silent. They didn't care if the Jews were exterminated. They *wanted* them to be exterminated.

It was Heine (d. 1856) who said of Judaism that it is not a religion but a misfortune. Then he had himself baptized. Heine understood Jewish being better than most; he was almost unique in his understanding of the Germans and their feelings about the Jews. Reading him makes it absolutely clear that the Germans' genocidal hatred of the Jews began very long before Adolf Hitler came to power in 1933. One might be forgiven for thinking it is in their DNA. Here are some extracts from a superb study of Heine by S. S. Prawer:[4]

- Heine refers to German nationalists discussing "what degree of non-German descent was necessary to qualify a man for execution when their 'new order' was established."

- "In the Goettingen beer cellar I once admired the thoroughness with which my Teutonic friends compiled proscription lists for the day on which they would come to power. Anyone descended (even unto the seventh generation) from a Frenchman, a Jew, or a Slav was condemned to exile…"

- Heine warns that one day the talisman of Christianity will lose its power to hold German brutality in check and "the savagery of the ancient warriors will burst forth once more, with that berserk rage of which Nordic tales and Nordic songs are so full".

Contrasting western Jews to their brethren from eastern Europe, Heine writes, "we no longer have the power to wear a beard, to fast, to hate, and to find in hatred the power to endure".

---

[4] S. S. Prawer, *Heine's Jewish Comedy* (Oxford: Clarendon Press, 1983), pp.163, 344, 256, 195.

My fellow-passengers are for the most part relatively young. I notice only three or four people who are old enough to belong to the generation of the murderers. On my way to the toilet I screwed up my eyes and stared hard at one of them, a slender, healthy and mean-looking man who wore a collar-less gray and green Bavarian jacket and had one of those awful green hats balanced on his knees. I wondered whether he intended to keep it there for all eight hours of the flight. In any event, I had the satisfaction of having him look away in response to my stare, and I counted that as a small victory: though a moment later felt a bit ashamed of myself.

Except for these old folk, everything around me here in the plane seems disconcertingly normal. But I know that the German "ordinariness" can mask deep treachery. There are people who can look you unflinchingly in the eye while saying the most astonishingly untrue or wicked things. Not all such people are German, of course, but I've met Germans who are very good at it. Albert Speer was one of them – telling me about his experiences as one of Hitler's inner circle, he paused to ask whether I would have a glass of beer with him. Leni Riefenstahl was another. When I asked her what the worst thing that ever happened to her was she replied almost instantaneously, as though with a well-rehearsed line, that it was when she learned, months after the war ended, what "they" had done to the Jews. And yes: she also told me, still looking me straight in the eye, that some of her best friends, like the directors Stroheim and Sternberg, were Jews.

This isn't Hannah Arendt's banality. It is cockiness, a challenge to see whether you have the strength of character to defy the conventions of polite and proper behavior and call these people's bluff. "Is it because of who I am that you wouldn't drink a glass of beer with me?" Speer asked as we waited in the lobby of his hotel for my taxi. What did he imagine, or hope, that I would say? "Of course not, Mr. Speer. I'd have loved to have a glass of beer with you on this hot summer's day, but I make a point of not drinking before sundown": something like that? What I did say, with a slight effort looking him directly in the eye, was "That's right. That's exactly why I couldn't drink with you." He looked very forlorn. "I understand, of course, because of what happened to your parents", he said with great sincerity, utterly missing the point that what happened to my parents was the least of the matter. "But there seems to be something else on your mind", I said, with a slightly hectoring, impatient, tone. "What is it?" He spoke so quietly and slowly that at first I couldn't make out what he was saying. I asked him to repeat what he'd just said. "I was wondering", I now heard him say, "whether you would shake my hand when you leave?"

I feel ashamed that I didn't challenge Riefenstahl. At the time it just didn't seem proper to suggest to this very old woman, no matter how obliquely, that she was lying to me. But of course, I should have done so, and I realized that almost immediately.

I've met the same quality in other Germans, most memorably in someone called Christoph Schramm. Schramm came to Bedales in 1955, when he and I were both about 15. His mother was an Englishwoman, the sister-in-law of Richard Musman, one of our French teachers. Musman had been a commando, and was wounded and captured by the Germans during the unsuccessful raid on Dieppe in the summer of 1942. He spent the rest of the war in a German prison. His sister-in-law, meanwhile, had married a German some time during the 1930's and remained in Germany until 1955, when she divorced her husband and took their son, Christoph, with her to England.

Schramm and I became best friends. After all we, and only we, had some kind of German-ness in common, though I'm not sure whether either of us had as yet learned enough of life to wonder what that might be. During a school vacation I visited him at his home in London. There, in his room, I saw that one wall was covered with magazine photographs of the actress Grace Kelly. These pictures belonged to me. I had had them on the wall above my bed in the school dorm, and someone had stolen them from there. I was quite upset about that - it was, I think the first time I'd ever had something of mine stolen. And now there was no getting round the fact that it was my good friend Schramm who had stolen them. Worse: he was evidently so confident of me that he hadn't bothered to remove the pictures before I came to visit him; he didn't care that I would be seeing them. I looked at him with goodness only knows what expression of anger and sadness on my face, and what I particularly remember was how he responded to it with a defiant grin and a shrug of his shoulders. I didn't have the self-respect or the guts to call him on this - I didn't even say anything about it - and to this day I still look back on my pusillanimity with shame. Neither of us ever referred to the pictures; our best friendship survived. But a few weeks later Schramm said I was a dirty Jew: and at least this time I walked away and never spoke to him again. All this happened about fifty years ago, and I still have not been able to let go of it.

Other instances that annoy the hell out of me: back in the early 1960's (I was living in Jerusalem in those days) Israel and Germany established diplomatic relations with each other. Many Israelis objected to this, and for several days there were demonstrations, editorials, speeches, denouncing the decision. When this tumult died down the Israeli public learned that Germany's first ambassador would be a man who had lost an arm fighting for the Fuehrer on the Russian front! There can have been few people in Israel who did not regard this choice as an affront. But despite the renewed demonstrations, the Germans did not put forward another man, and the Israel government accepted his credentials - as the Germans knew it would.

And now, most recently, I learn that for the 2006 World Soccer Cup games the German government is renovating the infamous stadium that Hitler built for the 1936 Olympics, and which is the setting for one of Riefenstahl's most famous propaganda movies.

The intention, to be sure, is not to celebrate Hitler and his movement. But it is – I have no doubt – to let the world know that Germany doesn't have to dissociate itself completely from its past and will decide for itself (thank you very much!) which aspects of that past it wants to live with. And if Germany decides to include Hitler's stadium of shame among the relics it is comfortable with, then there's nothing that anyone else can do about that. It's a neat *fait accompli*: after all, a person who objects to being there is welcome not to participate in the soccer championship.

I'm bothered by that silly business of staring down the old German. I hope I don't do that again. I've already told myself that I'm not going to get into debates or arguments with people in Germany – what would be the point? – and gimmicks like staring at people are at least as fruitless. What do I expect them to achieve? That I will make the mask fall off to reveal "the true" German who was wearing it? No. I would simply seem rude and perhaps a little unhinged.

And I know that in some cases there may actually be no mask there, and that any negativity I encounter is more likely to be in response to my rudeness than to my Jewishness. Well: at least in *some* cases!

Adam, calling from Hollywood to say goodbye, reminded me this morning that it is Hank's 21st birthday tomorrow. That in turn reminded me of Hank's visit to Germany a few years ago to visit a German girl – I think her name was Elisabeth – whom he had become intensely fond of when she was an exchange student at the Monument Mountain high school. Nominally – but we mustn't forget how deadly these *nomens* can become; under the Nuremberg Laws just one out of the four grandparents was enough to do the trick – nominally, Hank is one-half of a Jew, but in fact it is impossible to infer from his appearance or his conversation that he has any Jewish blood in him. Nevertheless, whatever residual

Jewishness clings to him or lingers, unacknowledged, in his gestalt was enough for this Elisabeth's grandparents to stay away from her parents' house when Hank visited her there. Nor, of course, did Hank and his girl visit the grandparents, even though they lived just a few blocks away. And I at least can't help wondering how much of these awful people's legacy has gone into the making of Elisabeth herself. Does she regard their attitude as just a little quirk? Does she perhaps share it in some degree? Or does she recognize her grandparents' vileness for what it is, and distance herself from them as a result? One might think that this experience would have been something of a wake-up call for Hank, but I don't know that it has been.

So, let me revise something I thought a few moments ago. There are some Germans who don't even bother to put on the mask – like Elisabeth's grandparents – and for some reason or the other I seem to want to let them know that I am here, alive, well and productive in their now no longer entirely *judenrein* Germany. (I understand that about 100,000 Jews live in Germany today. I find that quite appalling.) And there are other Germans who think that no one can recognize that they are wearing that mask – Speer and Riefenstahl are my exhibits A and B. I'd like to let some of them know that I'm onto them. And I suppose that in all fairness I must suppose that there are some Germans – a *very* few! – who are free from all this and have no need for a mask.

But why should I try to create a taxonomy along these lines? Deep inside me I think all Germans are tainted. The "good" Germans along with the rest of them. This conviction probably flies in the face of reason and decency. Yet it remains my conviction.

I keep on wishing that I understood what my trip here is all about. Do I perhaps want to confront German people with their shame? But what would that accomplish for me? Nothing, I should think! Certainly, nothing worthwhile came from my encounter with the Goldberg's German guest, Edith…

And yet there is something in me that feels that it is worth my while to show these people that I see them for what they are, and am not scared to let them know as much. Does that account for my decision to fly by Lufthansa and order kosher meals (I never eat kosher)? It all seems so pointless. And yet compelling! I have the disconcerting sense that I am being manipulated by someone inside me!

Goldhagen's book has been on my lap ever since I sat down, but largely hidden under the notebook in which I am writing. Nevertheless, a swastika or two will peek out from the book's marvelously vivid dustjacket. The stewardess came by a few moments ago to ask if I would exchange seats with the wife of the man next to me. I said I would, but only if they could provide me with another aisle-side seat. Which they couldn't. Again I had a disgraceful moment of satisfaction. I feel nervous about bringing out Goldhagen's book, fearful that other people would see what I am reading. But what if they did? What do I suppose they would do to me? Lynch me? I can't talk myself out of this funk, however, and the Goldhagen remains where it was – more or less concealed. I feel even more nervous about my kosher meal. How pathetic is that?

They are about to start serving dinner.

Question: why do we instinctively try to hide or downplay our Jewishness in public? As if - for many of us, at least - it wasn't altogether apparent to just about anyone! Are we embarrassed? Why should we be? Are we afraid of what will happen to us if people identify us as Jews? Is that why we often mouth the word "Jewish" *sotto voce*? Indeed, is that why Jews so seldom use the word "Jew", preferring instead to say "Jewish", as if this somehow mitigates the offense? Making Jews wear the yellow star on their clothing for all to see was one of the devilishly clever devices used by the Germans to torment Jews. It pulled the Jew out of his protective hiding: it "out-ed" him, as one might now say. The Nazis also knew that one way Jews have of trying not to be noticed is to give themselves "non-Jewish" names. Understanding the psychological power of stripping them of this disguise, the Nazis required every male Jew to take Abraham as his first name, and every woman, Sarah.

(I find it amusing that certain non-Jewish names - Sheldon or Sidney for example; there seems to be a preference for Tudor surnames - are chosen by so many Jews that they have become, in effect, Jewish names! There's a statement in the Koran that strikes me as an apt commentary on this: it reads something like, "They devised a device and their device devised against them". I also just remember a *midrash* that asks why some of our ancestors were not allowed to leave Egypt with Moses. The answer - an extraordinary one, really - "because they changed their names"!)

Of course, the very religious intentionally proclaim their Jewishness by the way they dress; and while there is much that I dislike about those people I do admire their dignity, their integrity, their fortitude, in being visibly and unambiguously what they are, even when what they are is scorned by the people among whom they live.

The steward handed me a tray – my dinner. I told him, perhaps a little too softly, that I had ordered a kosher meal. Nonplussed, he removed my *traif* tray and replaced it with a properly, rabbinically, certified one. "Oh it was you who ordered the kosher meal", he said in an entirely matter-of-fact tone. As if there was anyone else on the plane who might have done so!

Unfortunately, I had not thought to order an Atkins-compliant kosher meal, if there is such a thing. What I got instead was a morass of more or less inedible carbohydrates: Sabra brand eggplant sautéed in a tangy tomato sauce, for example, and a piece of chicken breast inextricably bonded to glutinous mashed potatoes and so relentlessly overcooked that, in its awfulness, it reminded of the cuisine of my grandmother, Dvorah, a fine woman who bore her many sufferings with sweetness and dignity but who was a ghastly cook. Also on my tray was a container of applesauce devoid of any discernible taste, and cookies with an ersatz but no doubt kosher yellow cream of stupefying sweetness. Each dish was wrapped in unusually thick aluminum foil, and so tightly sealed that at one point I thought I would hand back my repast uneaten. This gastronomic orgy, a bold label on each package told me, had been prepared by Borenstein Caterers of Jamaica, New York.

I hope they know that they owe me one!

My healthy, tanned, muscular German neighbor on the other hand ate his meal with demonstrative gusto, and I rather think that I saw just a little hint of a smile when he saw how little of my kosher food I ended up eating. Neither now nor at any point in the flight did we find occasion to talk to one another or even make eye contact.

I wonder why I have been to Germany so often. Three of my trips had their origin in the work that Florence Miale and I did on the Rorschach records of the major Nazi war criminals who were tried at Nuremberg. One of those criminals was Albert Speer. Florence and I had not found much to celebrate in his grotesque personality, and our findings were diametrically opposed to the published opinions of such heavyweights as Erich Fromm and Hugh Trevor-Roper, who regarded Speer as a genuine repentant. It occurred to me that since Speer had now finished serving his sentence, it might be useful to see whether the man we knew from his 1945 Rorschach really was different from the one whom Fromm, etc., perceived.

My interview succeeded in revealing some very dark and bizarre aspects of Speer's personality and, to my satisfaction at least, was consistent with our portrait of him in *The Nuremberg Mind*. This did not come as a surprise to either Florence or me. After all, the core of an individual's personality, his essential being, is not very much affected by the circumstances of his life (rather, it shapes his responses to those circumstances), and assuredly does not change because for opportunistic (in Speer's case) or other reasons he wishes it to.

But writing these words just now challenges me to confront myself with them. How many of my limitations – or the actions I have taken or wished I had taken - do I attribute to, or rather excuse by, "the circumstances of my life?"

Perhaps some other time!

My essay about Speer was published in many newspapers and magazines around the world (though by none in Germany), and caused something of a sensation. One day my agent at William Morris was asked by the editor of a magazine in Munich – the German edition of *Playboy* – whether I would care to do a series of interviews with other famous and interesting people, using the same psychological interviewing techniques I'd used with Speer.

I was both reluctant to write for a German magazine, and quite eager, for purely opportunistic reasons, I'm afraid, to do so. I'd recently been fired from Brooklyn College's political science department on the mere rumor that I'd done some work for the CIA; I had a small child to support; and both my morale and my bank balance were in urgent need of a boost. I tried to resolve my ambivalence about writing for the Germans by insisting on terms that were so unreasonable that they were bound to be refused. I would remain morally uncompromised, as a result, even if still broke and demoralized! My agent agreed to let me negotiate directly with the Germans, who paid for my travel expenses between New York and Munich.

In Munich I demanded an exorbitant amount for each article. I think the figure was $10,000. Much to my astonishment, the Germans agreed. I then said that I wanted all my travel expenses paid to anywhere in the world where there was someone I wanted to interview, and they agreed to that, and didn't flinch when I demanded the right to travel in any way I wanted – that included taking the Concorde across the Atlantic. They agreed to that. No negotiation has ever gone so smoothly for me. This was, I reckoned, an unanticipated form of German "making-good-again" (*Wiedergutmachung*), that being the astonishingly inappropriate term the Germans use to describe payments to Jews who suffered at their hands but survived. (I think that a concentration camp survivor gets something like $25 a year for each day he or she was imprisoned. Wow, does that work to make things good again!) But I'd never been much in favor of German making-good-again, and didn't want to become a recipient of it now; so as a last resort I played my trump card, confident that this would be the one demand they would refuse. I said that I wanted to begin the series with an interview with Leni Riefenstahl, Hitler's evil propagandist filmmaker. Neither the German *Playboy* nor any other German magazine had published my Speer article (no surprise, that) and it seemed reasonable to believe that they wouldn't want to publish one on another formerly illustrious person, either.

But they agreed to this condition, too. I signed the contract and returned to New York on a Concorde from London. A few weeks later I was back in Munich to see Riefenstahl.

She was even more awful than I'd imagined she would be. Even in her late eighties she was a beautiful woman, but she was also the crudest liar I've ever encountered. As the interview wore on I got the impression that she did not intend me to believe her lies but wanted to see whether I would challenge her on them. This, I'm ashamed to say, I did not do. In writing my essay about the interview it seemed essential that I avoid attacking her, or sounding shrill, and it was only after many drafts that I was able to present her remarks in a way that let readers draw their own conclusions about her. I faxed the article to the *Playboy* people in Munich.

Within hours I received a reply. It was curt. "We cannot publish your article. It is anti-German".

This was not the denouement I'd expected. I replied, "My article is about an evil person. A Nazi. It is anti-German only if you equate Germans and Nazis with each other. Surely, you would not want to do that?"

I never heard back from the Playboy people. My agent also wrote to them and he too did not receive a reply.

Berlin.

I slept much of the way north from Frankfurt and when I woke we were flying over Berlin's suburbs. What I could see from the plane looked altogether uninteresting except for a number of lakes; I assumed that one of them must be the infamous Wannsee, in a house on whose shores the administrative details of the Final Solution were worked out ("the Wannsee Conference"). But even with these associations, the view from the plane was, to borrow a term, a banal one. I tried to overlay it with the fantasy that I was in a Lancaster, or a B-26, with a full load of bombs to drop on the wicked city, but I didn't get very far with that.

Berlin turns out to be a dull, dusty and surprisingly shabby city. If it reminds me of any place I know it would probably be Tel Aviv. My hotel is in a fashionable area, just twenty yards or so round the corner from the Kurfurstendamm, one of the city's two principal streets. However, the hotel itself is anything but grand – it is more like a *pension* and my room is barely large enough to contain a small bed and desk. An inscription on the control panel of the hotel's elevator records that it was constructed by a firm called – SELZER! Which reminds me how indignant my father was when I once referred to it as a Jewish name. "It's a German name", he insisted with some passion. And of course, there's a lot of subtext in his reaction!

After unpacking my few things I went for a walk up the Kurfurstendamm, past the bombed-out Memorial church. I am very tired and not taking much in. The unsmiling faces on people all around intensify my weariness. It is difficult for me to imagine them glowing with joy and adulation as the Leader drives by in his open Mercedes. I am not at all interested in Berlin as a city, I have none of the tourist's eagerness, there are no sites I feel I must see. What am I doing here? I am not too tired to notice that a large proportion of the people I see are swarthy, presumably Muslim, types from Turkey, Morocco, etc. But I am also struck by how few racially-mixed people I have seen; and how few racially-mixed couples. I imagine that there's not much intermarriage between Aryans and Muslims. One very elderly man I saw, who was walking with remarkable vigor despite his age, had fencing scars on his cheeks. In the German aesthetic this used to be a mark of great distinction that betokened membership in an exclusive university fraternity in the days when dueling was an initiation rite. The practice was banned after the war by the occupying powers, but I wouldn't be surprised if it were to be revived at some point in the not-too-distant future. I remembered something I hadn't thought of for years, namely that Hans Morgenthau – a Jewish refugee from Frankfurt - also had fencing scars on his cheeks. It's hard to imagine him being admitted to an exclusive German fraternity, but perhaps there were Jewish fraternities that aped their betters by also having fencing as an initiation rite. I used to joke with Susan that her father probably got those scars while shaving.

On the Kurfurstendamm, returning to my hotel, I passed a shoe shop. Judging from the window display, its merchandise was expensive but not particularly fashionable. What particularly attracted my attention, however, was the shop's sign, a large illuminated sign, that read in part, "Budapester Schuhe . . . Qualitaet seit 1939". These few words suggested a number of interesting questions to me. I suspected that Budapest Shoes replaced a shop that had been in the same location before 1939, and that the earlier establishment had been owned by Jews and was confiscated by the Nazis – as all Jewish property was after the November 1938 Kristallnacht – and sold for almost nothing to one of the Party's racially- and ideologically-certified faithful? And who, I also wondered, would have been the customers for its expensive shoes in 1939, and the ensuing years? Perhaps the Party faithful and their ladies? Was it here that Himmler's boys in black, or at least those in the upper echelons, came for their jackboots? As I asked myself these questions Germany's past seemed to emerge, even if only briefly, from its cloacal hiding place. I also tried to deconstruct that phrase, *Qualitaet seit 1939* – "quality since 1939". It seemed to me that this was an essentially inflammatory statement. After all, there were other ways in which the shop's new owners could have conveyed the fact that it had been around for a while: *seit 1950*, for example, would have been sufficient for that purpose. So I found it impossible not to believe that that year – 1939 – had been identified for another purpose, which was to convey (not altogether discretely) a message about what the shop and its owners were really all about – that it had fallen into Aryan hands right after Kristallnacht. And understanding that message, I wondered how many Germans now make a point of buying their shoes here? And how few, for the same reason, make a point of not doing so? I thought that I ought to go into the shop and poke around a little, perhaps to catch a glimpse of its owner and customers. But I was tired and to tell the truth, the thought of doing that scared me a little.

As I write this in a sidewalk café next to the Burger King where I shall be going soon for some comfort food, a well-tailored Hassidic Jew, a young man, is walking in a great hurry up the Kurfurstendamm, his *tsitsis* and *peyes* bouncing up and down with each stride. Now, one of the main reasons why people sit in sidewalk cafes is to gaze at passers-by, and so I was surprised to see that no one even seemed to notice this very incongruous-looking young man. If I hadn't been so tired and had had more presence of mind I would have left some euros on the table and hurried after him - to note what other kinds of reactions his presence may have excited and, after I finally caught up with him, to ask him what on earth he was doing in this place.

This café is on the Kurfurstendamm, just round the corner from my hotel. I can't help thinking that it wasn't so long ago that Jews were freely terrorized on this street, humiliated and beaten; that Jewish shops were cordoned off, and slogans like "Germans don't buy from Jews" were painted on their windows. The buses driving up and down the street – Jews weren't allowed on them, not even if they sat at the back. Groups of Jews, with the yellow star conspicuous on their clothes, were marched down here, watched by stony-eyed throngs of Aryans lining the street, and disappeared for ever into police stations and concentration camps. And all this happened right where I was sitting, here on the Kurfurstendamm, during the adult lifetime of one in ten Germans who are still alive today.

I don't believe for a moment that this horrible past has been expunged - and not only because one in ten Germans alive today was part of it. I sense that the excremental currents of German history flow strong and deep just beneath the surface of the shabbiness and banality that is Berlin's reality today. What will it take for these currents to resurface ?

Someone could argue that I have no objective grounds, or only very few, for thinking this, and they would probably be right. But knowing that doesn't dispel these presentiments. Yet, on the other hand, the reality of Berlin today strikes me as so tangible, so self-evident, that it is not difficult to slide into an attitude that would have one suppose that this is all a fantasy, an unhealthy delusion about something that never happened, because things so grotesque *just do not happen*. Not ever!

History has a way of clinging to mankind as barnacles cling to a hull, impeding the progress that would deliver us from the past - an ugly and dysfunctional irritant that people try in vain to remove. But it seems to me too that we Jews are ourselves mankind's barnacle, an ugly and persistent reminder of its malevolence. We seem unable to change the vessel's course (though perhaps we are occasionally able to impede it a little) and indeed some part of us has conformed to the shape of its hull. But we survive every attempt to scrape us off. Belaboring this metaphor tells me that I am more tired, and distraught, than I have recognized. I'll order another beer before I go to bed, and forgo Burger King's comfort food.

It occurs to me that the non-Aryans I see everywhere, almost all of them from the lands of Islam, are nowadays a much larger proportion of Germany's population than we Jews ever were. If as many Jews were now living in Germany - heaven forfend that they should - and were as visible as the Muslims are, the murders would already be well under way. But it seems that in Germany today a large and largely uneducated and unemployed Muslim population is far more acceptable than a much smaller and far more productive Jewish population had been. It's unfair that only we and not our replacements on these streets have had to suffer so greatly at the hands of the Germans! Let them experience some of our misery. Why should we be alone in this?

These shameful, terrible thoughts just passed through my mind. I'll blame them on my fatigue and the German beer. But they lead me again to ask, what am I doing here? What chimera am I pursuing? I'll rescue myself with the thought that were it not for our suffering - our redemptive suffering perhaps: oh no, that's also a can of worms! - the Germans would not feel inhibited about venting their hatred and frustration on their "guests" (as they call them) from the Muslim lands. But it seems inevitable to me that at some point in the perhaps not very distant future the Germans will be ready for a repeat performance. The inhibitions they feel today will disappear without a trace.

But perhaps the Germans *have* become less willing to murder masses of people they don't like. Perhaps Germans *have* finally left their *Sonderweg* – the "Special Way" as they call the uniquely ugly course that their history followed for so many years. But these possibilities, which frankly I wouldn't bank on, don't always inhibit the Germans from following a *Sonderweg* when they consider that history. Their leader today, Chancellor Schroeder, is adamant that Germans should no longer apologize for their past! And what is one to make of his unspeakable cynicism in thanking the American, British, French and Russian leaders, on the 60th anniversary of VE-Day recently, for having "liberated" the German people from the Nazis? Most Germans seem to function as though they are sealed off from their Nazi past – it has nothing to do with them, it is not part of their daily lives or of their cultural memory, it is not something for which they bear responsibility or need to feel shame. And their success in isolating themselves – insulating themselves – from their gruesome past means that they have not learned the important lessons and that increases the likelihood of all this coming to the fore again. "Renunciation without aversion is not lasting", as Gandhi liked to say; and of course, no aversion is possible for the Germans if they avoid facing up to what they should be renouncing.

I hate that. I want all Germans to live in the immediate, haunting presence of their nation's crimes.

But really, why should they? Don't we all let ourselves get away with a lot? And what benefits have all my raging and grieving and endless astonishment brought me? Should other persecuted people – Blacks in America, Armenians in the Middle East, and endlessly on and on – also feel the same way? What would the world be like if people didn't put behind them grievances about events long ago? Or is our Jewish experience unique? Is it perhaps the appalling history of our suffering and the more-than-theoretical likelihood of its recurrence in the future, that give us license to fan the flames of others' guilt and shame? But if that is so we can no longer single out the Germans for what they did to us – they are merely the most recent of our tormentors, the heirs to a tradition that began with Pharaoh and will end only when the Messiah comes.

I'd like to have a clearer understanding of the distinctiveness of the Holocaust. Several years ago, at my house in Jerome, Arizona, I read the text of an order that the Secretary of the Army in Washington sent in the 1880's to a General Crook, commander of U.S. Army troops in Arizona Territory, instructing him *in haec verba* to "exterminate . . . the savages". Of course I knew that many nations have been wiped off the face of the map - the Biblical record shows that our own ancestors themselves engaged in repeated acts of "ethnic cleansing" as it is called nowadays. But to see the word "exterminate" used with complete candor, and to facilitate the deed by reducing people to the category of "savages" was really chilling. To this day a road outside Camp Verde is called "General Crook Trail" and a path in Arlington National Cemetery is also named for him. He must have done his job well.

Over and over again I have made forays into the Nazi world. I think at bottom my purpose was twofold: to convince myself, to really convince myself, that these unbelievable events actually happened; and to expose myself to whatever little portion of the victims' pain and suffering I can encounter. But I don't think that this has helped me to resolve anything. An aura of improbability still clings in my mind, to these horrors (I am not of course denying that they occurred; but at some level it seems to me impossible to believe that human beings could behave like the Germans did); and I cannot pretend that I have felt more than a minute particle of what the victims experienced. But these forays have helped me to become bitter and obsessive – not just about the Germans, but also the British and the Americans, in particular, who could have done so much to save Jews: but with an easy shrug, declined the opportunity. I once asked Harold Macmillan, why the allies hadn't bombed the railroad tracks leading to Auschwitz, the gas chambers, the crematoria – and he replied earnestly that I should be assured that Britain wanted to defeat the enemy as quickly as possible, in part to prevent more Jews from being murdered. I had a similar answer from – well, I can't remember his name just now – but he was the person in the Department of War who vetoed the idea of sending American planes to bomb Auschwitz. He told me this from the splendor of his huge suite of offices in the Chase Manhattan headquarters in downtown Manhattan, where he was employed (at a fat salary, I'm sure) as an "adviser" to the bank and to the Rockefellers.

However, I think about the British and American role in the Holocaust only occasionally, and I don't hold today's Britons and Americans at all culpable. Should I regard them with the same hatred as I do the Germans? Isn't someone who facilitates murder also responsible for the crime? Obviously, my exemption of the British and Americans is illogical: but there we are.

My bitterness and anger about the Germans have made it easy for me to keep the world at bay, to be outside and mistrustful. In a way this is another victory for them (not that they would care, or even take note of it) – a Jew who is conscious of the Holocaust cannot have a full life, and can be sure of so little. I don't think that the nice German people promenading up and down the Kurfurstendamm have this burden. Their cold cynicism and easy restructuring of truth keep them far from it. I understand that the French take the radioactive waste from their nuclear power plants and turn it into glass bricks which they bury deep underground. The Germans have a pretty radioactive history, don't they, and they pack it up nice and tight so that they don't need to pay attention to it. The poison is all buried.

But that of course means that it still exists. Nothing is buried so deeply that it can't be disinterred, even from that foreign land which is the past:

> *They set out each day on bulldozers of shame,*
> *To level the contours of that foreign land.*
> *But the mountains of sorrow will not yield;*
> *They rise from ravines of death where the names are,*
> *The faceless names.*

I just remembered now that when I was looking for a place to stay on this trip I found something called the HEP Hotel. HEP is itself a pretty radioactive word. It is an acronym for *Hierosolyma est perdita* – Jerusalem is destroyed – and goes back to at least the eleventh century as a cry used by anti-Semites to cover the gamut of their predilections, from inciting pogroms to merely humiliating Jewish passers-by. (Herzl's biographers record how deeply he was affected by hearing it.) It doesn't really matter whether or not the owners of the hotel knew what this word means, though I'm struck by the fact that they write it in upper case – HEP – (rather than Hep), which suggests that they think of it as an acronym. Either way, HEP is a little strand that binds this hotel and its owners to Germany's gruesome history. The past is not merely a foreign land.

* * * *

In the lobby there's a PC connected to the Internet for the use of guests. I sent a short email home, and then did a little bit of surfing. I discovered that in Germany the Nazis have a somewhat furtive Internet presence. Google will only let you into sites found with a "Nazi" or "Hitler" or similar search term if you enter a password; but I couldn't find out how one goes about obtaining one. I am against this kind of censorship. Let the Nazi dream re-emerge, I say, from the sewers in which it is presently sheltering, so that it can be brutally and perhaps "finally" smacked down again.

I also learned that according to a 2004 survey 36% of Germans hold anti-Semitic attitudes. This is the highest percentage in Europe. Yessir, the past is still here, no matter how securely they think that they've locked up the Internet! According to another survey, 62 per cent of Germans are "sick of all the harping on about German crimes against the Jews".

Of course they are. As we say, the Germans will never forgive us for the Holocaust

Day Two

A tourist bus makes a circuit of about 10 stops around Berlin, and with a single ticket one can get on and off at each of them. I thought that this would be as convenient a way as any to get to the Jewish Museum which, it is worth noting, is tucked away in a pretty remote part of town. It isn't a building you chance upon. You have to intend to go there.

One enters the museum into a building that used to be the Prussian Court of Appeals. An ironic choice, this, associating the memory of all those dead Jews with an institution that, deaf to their appeals, had affirmed that they no longer possessed any rights at all. At the ticket desk a pretty girl of Oriental appearance looked doubtful when I said that I wanted a senior ticket, and asked to see some identification. I said no, that she would have to take it on trust that I am 60 or more; and since this kind of silly adamancy is itself probably a mark of advancing years she didn't press the point further and sold me the senior ticket. I went upstairs to see an exhibition about the firm of Topf, whose contribution to the genocide was the design and construction of the high-quality crematoria used at Auschwitz and elsewhere. The exhibit includes ledgers, blueprints, correspondence relating to this work. One photograph showed a hall full of men hard at work on their drafting boards, and an actual drafting board, similar in appearance to the ones in the photograph, stood alongside it. Somewhat incongruously (because it didn't seem to have been made by Topf), there was also a square, rather weather-worn, wooden hatch, reinforced with a couple of iron bands, from the roof of a gas chamber at Auschwitz. It was through this hatch that Germans dropped pellets of Zyklon B down into the chamber crammed with naked Jews. I stood for a long time looking at this foul object. It was difficult to believe that so drab and humble a thing played a significant role in a hugely terrible moment in history. I tried but failed to imagine the sounds that came from below when the hatch was raised. I wondered whether the SS man who dropped the pellets through it ever acknowledged the enormity of his simple little act. What thoughts would pass through his mind? Perhaps that if he hurried, he'd be able to have a cup of coffee before returning to work again? Was he possibly irritated at those dirty Jews for making so much noise? Or did he congratulate himself on his good fortune in having such a cushy job?

You enter the other part of the museum by descending a steep flight of steps, at the bottom of which you have the choice of going along one of two corridors, both with a slight upward tilt - an echo, unwitting or otherwise, of the kabalistic doctrine of *aliyah m'toch yeridah*, ascent through descent. The exhibitions in one corridor are about Jews who have been killed, in the other about Jews who escaped the Nazis – the so-called "exiles", as the Germans like to call them. I find that term offensive. Exiles can look forward to returning to the place that was their home. Germany has shown that it was never a home for Jews. You would have to be a pretty messed-up person to consider ending your "exile" by "returning" there.

Set into the walls of these corridors are illuminated, glass-fronted display cases. The displays do not offer an overview of the Holocaust. Rather, they focus on an individual or a small family, and include not only photographs but letters and all sorts of everyday personal effects. The intention evidently is to move us from trying to comprehend six million people, an impossible task, to an encounter with one or two Jews at a time, whom we are now able to recognize as distinct individuals. It was well done. One of the corridors ends with a heavy steel door that is opened for you by an attendant. Going through that door, which looks very unfriendly, is itself slightly chilling. It leads into a very tall windowless chamber that rises up (perhaps 40 or 50 feet) from an irregularly-shaped polygonal floor. There is nothing in the chamber, and every face of it is in stark grey concrete. I have never been in a more silent place: here however the silence was not tranquil, but conveyed intense horror and sadness, as if pure, raw emotion had been mixed into the concrete of which it is constructed. In a way it tells a visitor all that he or she needs to know. I left much sooner than I'd expected to, actually sobbing as I walked down the corridor that had brought me there.

I calmed myself with deep breathing and continued up the other corridor. There were very few Jewish people here, as far as I could tell, other than a group of Israeli teenagers (why on earth had they come to this benighted country?) With *goyim* all around me, I had a proprietary feeling, as though the grief belongs to me, as though I own it, and that a certain deference is due to me both directly and as a representative of all those murdered and wounded people: an acknowledgement, perhaps, of the nobility to which our suffering has elevated us. I record what I felt. This is not a point of view I would reach by reflecting on the facts, or that I would to justify. It is, to be sure, entirely invalid. But it did lead me to demand of myself what, really, have I suffered at the hands of the Germans, what specific injuries, what distortions of my life...

With concentration camp pictures all around me, and the faces of murdered and "exiled" Jews shining with light and life - even happy faces – what else could I answer but "nothing"? I've not actually suffered at all. Over the years I've had brief moments when I wish that I had been imprisoned in a concentration camp (though with the proviso that I'd survive!) *That* would have been real suffering. But here in the museum it seemed sacrilegious to think that I am a victim of the Germans.

Acknowledging this, I felt an intense sense of loss, almost the erosion of my very self: as if a large and essential slice of my being had just been excised. Presently, though, I recognized that there is no virtue in being a victim, and that surviving a genocidal concentration camp entitles one to very little, if anything: except for the question which I suspect is often asked with an undertone of skepticism: "how *did* you survive?", by which in fact is really meant, "And what did you do in order to survive?"

Yet . . . I am a victim. Albeit indirectly, the Germans are responsible for the disruption of my life when I was a very small child, for the distorted personalities of my parents, for much of the sadness and anger I feel as someone who *knows* that he belongs to and cannot escape from belonging to (even if he wished to, which he doesn't) a people that has been persecuted, despised, humiliated, tortured and finally, murdered. I am a victim of Germans, too, because of the obscene, self-betraying, connection I feel to them, this being an attachment that is in no way reciprocated, but that has hindered me from forming more acceptable ones, has limited my capacity to feel that I have roots I can trust, that leads me to doubt that there is any place in which I can feel secure, let alone at home: and that is why I always, everywhere, feel less than sufficiently connected to the people around me. And now, here in the Jewish Museum, how can I not see myself in the faces, seemingly so full of life, in those photographs? But what satisfaction is there in being connected with all these murdered people? I am feeling very lonely just now and wish my wife was here with me. But if she were here she would try to make me feel better, and I didn't come here to feel better.

I don't want to interrupt my train of thought, but I do want to mention one other part of the museum that I found intensely affecting. As I approached the end of a corridor, on one of the upper floors of the new building, I heard bursts of a strange, clinking sound. One wall of the corridor opened up into a space that was visible only when you stood more or less in front of it, a dark and irregularly-shaped space, on the floor of which there were thousands of stylized faces, about ten inches long, made of iron, strewn around more or less randomly to a depth of about a foot or so. One is invited to walk into this space, which of course means that one treads on these faces, and in doing so one makes the clinking sound I had heard moments earlier. It is not difficult to hear those sounds as the agony cries of the Germans' victims: of tens of thousands of them, of hundreds of thousands of them - of millions of them. Those sounds ought to haunt the souls of every German, and remind them of the murdered ones; but no less, it ought also to haunt the souls of every Jew who is no longer - or perhaps never was – sufficiently attentive to his people's torment.

In taking stock of what effect the Germans have had on my life I should also remember the stories I heard of the brutality that members of my family experienced at the hands of the Germans. I heard these stories when I was a child, and they are part of what I grew up with, therefore part of who I am. They have shaped my outlook on life, and have informed my recognition of what is possible in this life. The impression they made on me was so intense that I believe I can remember them more or less as they were told to me by my parents.

Here's one of those stories, pretty much as it was told to me by my father (except of course for the passage I downloaded from the Internet.)

The man (I don't know his name) was a cousin of my paternal grandfather, Moishe. Like Moishe, he had left Poland at the beginning of the twentieth century and settled in Germany. When World War I broke out he enlisted in the German army, although he was not a German citizen, and performed some heroic deeds, for which he won a medal that was awarded only for deeds of exceptional valor. In 1937 my grandfather left Germany and emigrated to Palestine. His cousin however decided to remain in Germany. He was confident that his status as a war hero would safeguard him and his family.

In November 1938, the month of Kristallnacht, the German government rounded up 17,000 Polish Jews living in Germany –

men, women and children - and expelled them to Poland at a border crossing near the village of Zbaszyn. The Jews were expelled from Germany - but after the first few people crossed into Poland the border guards, acting on orders from the Polish government, refused to allow any more in. (All of the Jews were Polish citizens.) This was in November, when the brutal central-European winter was already setting in. Using the internet connection at my hotel, I found this description of what happened then:

> *"The deportees had to walk the last seven kilometers of the main deportation route (Berlin-Posen) to the border station Zbaszyn. If anyone was unable to carry their luggage or fell behind their luggage was taken from them and thrown away. Those who did not keep up were beaten... A distressing report describes how the SS drove the deportees into the river that formed the border. The Polish border guards followed them and after wandering about for hours finally began a dispute with the SS about to whom these Jews belonged."*

The Jews remained trapped in the no-man's land between the two countries, for the most part without food or shelter. We don't know how many of them died, but it seems that most of them did. The records show that of about 1000 Jews from Hamburg, just 200 survived. If that is representative of the mortality rate among all of the Jews at Zbaszyn, and subtracting perhaps one thousand Jews in the groups that were admitted at the outset, one must assume that over twelve thousand of the deportees died.

Among them were my grandfather Moishe's war-hero cousin, his wife and children.

And then there's this story, that my mother told me – it concerns *Tante* Greta, one of her seven aunts.

Tante Greta was a simple, happy person. Her life revolved around her husband; the couple was childless. One day the Gestapo came for him – just like that. They came for him because he was a

Jew. It's possible that they accused him of a crime, but if so it was surely a trumped-up charge, because he was a good man. "Don't worry yourself too much", he assured Tante Greta as they took him away. "I'll be back tomorrow". Well, of course, tomorrow came and went, but Tante Greta's husband did not return home. She went to the Gestapo headquarters to find out when her husband would be released, and was told to come back the next day. The next day they brushed her off again. She brought his pills, and the Gestapo man promised to give them to him. He told her to come back the next day, and on the next day he told her the same - this went on for a couple of weeks, with the Gestapo officials becoming increasingly rude and hostile on each visit. But then, one day, she was greeted with a warm welcome and promised that her husband would be returning home that Friday. "Just in time for your Sabbath" the man said. "Go home and make some good chicken soup for him!'

For the next two days she scrubbed and polished the rooms of their modest house. She did the laundry. She prepared her husband's favorite food. She baked *challah*, the Jewish bakery having been closed down by the Nazis. She set the table with their best dishes and silverware that, probably, were not all that fine but seemed to her the last word in elegance, and she plucked some flowers from her garden and arranged them in a cut-glass vase on the table. She stepped back and thought – "He's going to be so happy to be home, so happy to see how beautifully I have prepared our Sabbath meal!

It was now nearly seven o'clock; the sun would be setting – and the Sabbath would begin – in less than half an hour. It hadn't occurred to her that the Gestapo would not live up to their promise to bring him home, but now she worried about that and sat anxiously at the kitchen table waiting for the sound of the door knocker.

And then she heard it. There were people at her front door! She sprang up, saw that she still had her apron on and took it off hurriedly, puffed up her thinning hair in the mirror in the hallway and opened the front door with a happy smile on her face.

Three Gestapo men were at the door, and they too were smiling. The one in the center of their small group, the one who had promised Tante Greta that he would bring her husband home, stepped forward with a gaily-wrapped box for her. Her first thought, "How nice these men are. A box of chocolates for all the trouble they've caused us."

"I promised I'd bring your husband home" the Gestapo man said, still with the smile on his face. "Here he is". He handed her the box. Tante Greta must have looked perplexed, because a moment later he said, "Or rather, his ashes!"

The Gestapo men doubled over with laughter and strolled casually back to their car. Tante Greta was found a few hours later by two of her sisters, covered in ashes and whimpering unintelligibly. She never regained her sanity and a few months later was a victim of the Nazi's euthanasia program.

Forty or fifty or maybe one hundred or two hundred other members of my family were also murdered by the Germans. The family tree my father drew for me is very wide - three and four generations back people in my family had lots of children; but most of them were killed by the Germans, and so the tree for the most recent is as narrow as it had earlier been wide.

I left the Jewish Museum feeling that I was emerging from my ghetto refuge into a hostile world. The bus took me through parts of the former East Berlin, including the infamous Karl Marx Allee and past a most forbidding-looking diplomatic enclave (the US embassy was still being built) to the official German Holocaust memorial.

It is notable, I think, that this memorial was only opened a few months ago – sixty years after the conquest – or "the liberation", as the conquered now prefer to say - of Germany. It covers an area about as large as a football field and consists of concrete slabs of different sizes (though none more than about 5 feet tall) crammed next to each other, seemingly at random. If the purpose here is to have us recall that the Nazis went after Jews long and short and tall indiscriminately, the point is noted. But what is far more notable, it seems to me, is that the overwhelming impression conveyed by these slabs is of complete impersonality, of drab uniformity. Stubby gray concrete cubes after all are not exactly evocative of human beings. But perhaps it works for Germans. Indeed, I think that the monument evokes what the Germans thought of the Jews they murdered far more vividly than it evokes the murdered Jews themselves. And perhaps a memorial to the crimes, that is to say a memorial of the murderers, has more value than a memorial to the people they murdered.

At the opening ceremony for the memorial the speaker of the Bundestag said something to the effect that the memorial proves that Germany is facing up to its history. Right! I remember reading somewhere that because Jewish monuments in Germany today are frequently defaced with anti-Semitic graffiti, it was decided to coat the slabs of the Holocaust Memorial in Berlin with a compound that would resist paint. The builders of the memorial contracted with a company called Degussa to supply this compound, but later it turned out that Degussa is a subsidiary of the corporation that supplied Auschwitz and other camps with Zyklon-B pellets. You profit by helping to kill the Jews, it would seem, and then you profit by protecting the memorials to them from people who would like to see even more Jews killed! In due course, I think, the contract was cancelled and some other corporation – perhaps an untainted one; no doubt there are such – got the job of protecting the concrete slabs from the present!

I had no desire to walk through this drably dead place, so I stayed on the bus and noted the Brandenburg Gate, which is more or less opposite the Holocaust Memorial and, just beyond that, the Reichstag – sorry, the Bundestag – and Schroeder's Chancellery. I've been to capital cities before, but I have never seen one that is as desolate and empty as this one. There are huge straight streets, even huger empty spaces (for one of which Speer had designed his appalling "Germania"; it remains empty, as though still waiting for what it had once been promised), and very few people. Indeed, I am struck by how altogether empty of people most of Berlin seems to be. I've been in three or four places where people congregate but, aside from them, one can drive for miles through the heart of Berlin and see hardly a soul on the sidewalks. Very strange. And this emptiness reinforces the dismayingly dismal light and the eerie silence all around one. Quite coincidentally, I am struck by how few churches there seem to be here.

The map of Berlin shows any number of streets and squares named after Jews who are no longer with us – there's a Walter Benjamin Platz, for example; Ben Gurion and Yitzhak Rabin have their streets. There is even a Hannah Arendtstrasse; which however is in a separate part of town from Heideggerstrasse. (Heidigger, of course, despite his great stature as philosopher, was a virulent Nazi ideologue and led the drive to make Germany's universities *Judenrein*. And he was the despicable Arendt's lover!) I discovered that there is a Marlene Dietrich Platz, too. Marlene was not a Jew but she was one of the miniscule number of overtly and bravely anti-Nazi Germans. I remember that some years after the war ended, it may have been in the 1960's, she summoned up the courage (if that's what it was) to go to Germany and give a concert here in Berlin. She was booed off the stage by people who resented her for her anti-Nazi activities. What can one say?

* * * *

I took the bus all the way back to the stop on the Kurfurstendamm where I had picked it up earlier this morning. Although I'd eaten lunch in the Jewish Museum I was feeling hungry again. I found an empty table at one of the sidewalk cafés and ordered an omelet and a large Pils. I'm feeling very tense and angry. The waiter gave me the check intended for the Swiss couple at the table next to me, and gave them mine. It took him a remarkably long time to understand the problem, and so the Swiss man and I took settled the matter by simply handing each other the correct checks. "That didn't seem very difficult to me", he said, smiling. "No", I replied. "German efficiency seems a bit of a myth. Probably why they lost the war!" A stupid thing to say, I know, but the Swiss couple thought – or pretended to think – that this was very funny. When they left I again was overcome by spontaneous doubts about my sanity – did this unbelievable event, this murder on an unparalleled scale, really happen? And was I really connected to it? Life usually feels too ordinary for one to incorporate such extraordinary horrors into one's awareness. And then I asked myself: am I up to all this: whatever *this* really is? Do I really want to continue here? Why shouldn't I just take a cab to the airport and catch the next plane to Boston? I remain obsessed by my recognition of how astonishing it is that six million Jews were murdered: it is literally, or almost literally, an incredible fact - as though it didn't occur in any of our four dimensions, but in one of the others envisaged by the string theorists. And I am also obsessed by how difficult for me it is to recognize that this city was the place from which the murders were encouraged, organized, legitimized: and in which quite a few of them were actually carried out. Why can't I hear the shrieks? Feel the terror? Sense the murderous hatred? There is such a disconnect between what happened then and the totally unremarkable reality of this city today. I wonder what might be able to bridge the two. History? Truth? No, anyone can see that these are insufficient. I think that the only viable bridge to this horrible past is one of intense emotion, but for now I don't want to pursue that further. And talking about things I don't want to talk about: Oh how I would love to have been a GI here in the summer of 1945. I would have made the savagery of the Soviet troops in

Berlin pale by comparison! But in what capacity would I have inflicted my vengeance? Merely as a Jew? As the relative of so many murdered Jews? No, I think that perhaps I would have done what I would do as the unappeasable outrage of the person to whom they would have done what they would have done had they been able to. And this is what it comes down to, in the end: it is my - my entirely personal, insatiable - astonishment and outrage. I'm no emissary for the Jewish people, or for the murdered Jews. It is me - and millions of other "me's"- whom the Germans have so unforgivably outraged. In considering their inhumanity it would be obscene for me self-righteously to consider myself too good to respond to those swine in kind. And I would hate myself if I were unable to do that – if I were unable to murder or torture even a single one of them. In my notebook, waiting to be gleaned at harvest-time, I have the following passage from Hazlitt's essay, "On the pleasure of hating" : "We learn to curb our will and keep our overt actions within the bounds of humanity . . . but cannot part with the essence or principle of hostility... hatred alone is immortal". Perhaps that is the bridge for which I've been looking. It's a rude, crude, unlovely structure, to be sure but one that functions and is indestructible. I suspect, though with some regret, that I would have forced myself to keep my actions "within the bounds of humanity". I'm a Jew, after all...

In my notebook there is also a quote from Prawer's study of Heine. Contrasting himself and other Western Jews to East European Jews, Heine writes, "we no longer have the power to wear a beard, to fast, to hate, and to find in hatred the power to endure".

Well, *I* have a beard...

Day Three

There is a very substantial breakfast buffet in the hotel's narrow little dining room, though I suspect it offers the same assortment every day. I feel acutely that I am surrounded in this cramped space by Germans. They are all busy eating, or going to the buffet to help themselves to more food, or reading their papers – no one seems to talk, however, though everyone looks up each time a person enters the room. There are several waitresses, whose task is to clear the table, to restock the buffet, and to ask whether one wishes for coffee or tea. The waitress who offered me this choice today is Indian, from the South, and dark. Her German is fluent but not, I suspect, ample; and I notice that while the other waitresses gather in little clusters and whisper to one another while they survey the room – as though they were the audience in a theater – she remains by herself. She looks vaguely familiar, and it bothers me that I can't understand why. But after I left the dining room I realized that she reminded me of my mother's cousin Ilse. Or, I should say, an Indian variant of Ilse. I hadn't thought about Ilse, her husband Erwin, or their daughter Eva in – I imagine – two or three decades. But it is useful to remember them now.

I knew all three of them as rather sweet and gentle people, eager to like and be liked, and perhaps not as intelligent as most other people in my family. Erwin had been a judge in Danzig. When all Jews were expelled from the German legal system he was sent to a concentration camp – it was probably Dachau. He was released after a while, and returned to his family. My parents helped them to emigrate to India, which they reached shortly before the war broke out. Eva would have been about five then. They were not interned when the war broke out, and remained in Kashmir, where Erwin managed the orchards of a maharaja who was one of my father's patients. Eva went to the same American-run boarding school in the Himalayas as I, and then moved to England, where she became a nurse, married a Gentile, and disappeared somewhere below the radar. Erwin and Ilse stayed on the farm, quite poor, very isolated, and (I imagine) increasingly anxious about how they would support themselves when they were too old to work. One day a German diplomat arrived at the orchard, and invited Erwin and Ilse to the German embassy in New Delhi to meet the ambassador, who was anxious to discuss their plans for the future. When they went to Delhi the ambassador offered Erwin a job at the embassy – a job, moreover, that would be considered a posting from Bonn, and thus would entitle Erwin to a (German) diplomatic passport and all the trimmings that went with it. Erwin accepted, and in no time at all he and Ilse were part of the German diplomatic family in New Delhi. He retired several years later and went "back" with Ilse to spend their remaining days in the Fatherland. Once, when I was in Lahore for the summer holidays, my mother suggested that we spend a few days in Delhi. We stayed with Heinz, a Swiss-born architect who'd lived in Delhi for decades; visited a number of people (including the Maharajah of Patiala, I remember); had lunch with a brigadier who told us that, as a Jew, he would not be able to rise any higher in the Indian army; went to the bazaars near the Red Fort where Georgian silver was sold by the weight; and spent most of the rest of our time with Erwin and Ilse. One afternoon, I was obliged to accompany Ilse and my mother to the swimming pool in the German diplomatic compound. I was struck by the deference shown to Ilse by the diplomats' wives. They found her every remark unprecedentedly witty; her every observation profound and original; and proof of her standing as an aesthete of the first order in her every comment about the loveliness of the flowers in the garden, the sari of a female servant, or the pleasant weather. Ilse, guileless and child-like as she was, lapped this all up, and every now and then looked at my mother with what I fancied was a triumphant "*these* people don't think I'm that dumb!" expression in her eyes. As far as Ilse appeared to be concerned, it had all been "made good again".

I went for a long walk and came to the KDW department store on the Kurfurstendamm. The taxi driver who brought me from the airport had told me that the KDW is one of Berlin's finest landmarks, and tourist brochures in the hotel also made much of it. However, today is Sunday, and the store was closed. But from the outside at least, and judging by the displays in its windows, KDW seemed to me to be much like any other large department store, and certainly not a place of any consequence. Later, in the hotel, I went to the store's website to see if I could discover what the excitement is all about, and I learned there that KDW is Europe's largest department store, which did not seem to me to be a particularly notable fact; I also learned, however, from hyped-up banners on almost every page of the site, that in two years' time KDW will be celebrating its centenary. To flesh out this momentous milestone the site includes a chronology of the most notable events in each year since the store opened in 1907. And here matters became rather more interesting.

For one, the chronology is full of errors, and these seem to me to reflect the ineptitude that permeates modern Germany. No one back home is going to believe me when I say that the Germans today are inefficient and incompetent. We think of them as epitomes of competence, rather, even though they now have the highest unemployment rate in western Europe and a pitifully stagnating economy.

Noting Gandhi's Salt March of 1931 and his assassination in 1948, the KDW historians refer to him as Mohandas Karamchod Gandhi. His middle name was, of course, Karamchand, and I can't be the only person in Germany today who knows that in Hindi and other Indian and Pakistani languages *chod* means - fuck! I'd like to think that the famously celibate Mahatma would have found this misstatement a little droll. This faux pas was followed by another - KDW has a President J. Edgar Hoover officially opening the Empire State Building in 1931. Even the chronology of German history is presented inaccurately - we are told that the militarization of the Rhineland occurred in 1931, when of course it took place in 1936: anyone should know that the maneuver was ordered by Hitler and that he came to power in 1933.

But back to KDW's chronology. One memorable event passed over in silence was the Nazis' confiscation of KDW from its Jewish owners. I imagine that that probably happened in the aftermath of the Kristallnacht, but I don't know and it really doesn't matter, does it? The KDW team shows impressive delicacy in the way they discuss the notable events of "those years". "Hitler" and "Nazi" never sully this chronology. For 1933, the year when the Nazis took control of Germany, the chronology records only, "Reichstag fire and books burned in Berlin" - we are not given the identity of the arsonists. The next, equally oblique, reference to the Nazis appears in the chronology for 1939, which carries the cryptic entry, "Beginning of World War 2". 1940 is noted only as the year the new Dalai Lama was recognized; 1941, for a production of Brecht's *Mother Courage*; 1942, for the release of the movie, *Casablanca*. (The implication is that *Mother Courage* and *Casablanca* were shown in Berlin, which of course would have been impossible. Brecht was an anti-Nazi Marxist, and *Casablanca* an overtly anti-Fascist movie.) It is not until 1943 that we are reminded of the war, and then only with an entry that reads, in its entirety, "Berlin and KDW destroyed by Anglo-American bombing" (also an inaccuracy; lamentably or otherwise, Berlin was never entirely destroyed, and a great deal of it was still standing before the Russian attacks in 1945). The only event noted for 1944 is that a German scientist won the Nobel Prize for Chemistry; and then, for 1945, we are back to the real world with the statement, "World War 2 ends with the capitulation of

Germany" – which is also inaccurate, since the war didn't end until the capitulation of Japan three months later.

I wonder how many Germans read this chronology and accept it as gospel because they know no better: and how many, recognizing its evasions and distortions, nod their heads sympathetically - and show their solidarity by making a point of going to KDW the next time they have some shopping to do. Oh those poisonous years! If I'd been running KDW I'd simply have discarded the chronology in its entirety. I mean, why even go there? Or perhaps I'd have copied the example of the Budapest Shoe Shop down the road with its bland, "Quality since 1939" - a statement too concise to offend and yet redolent of so much evil. Whether they know it or not, the KDW people act as though by trivializing non-German history (President J. Edgar Hoover, indeed!) no one will notice the specific slice of German history that they have excised from the record. But these ploys, this fiddling with facts, this highhandedness, can only take the Germans so far. Their past is not "a foreign land" - it's a filthy neighborhood they have to live in even though they'd love to move elsewhere: and that's an intractable problem for them. They're damned if they deny or distort their history, and they are shattered if they acknowledge it for what it is. But I needn't worry about all that. It's their problem. Not mine.

Beyond the KDW is a large, desolate-looking square. As I walked around it I was approached by an emaciated young woman who asked me for a euro or two. Her speech was slurred and she looked very unhealthy: I guessed that she was a drug addict. I felt a little guilty about not helping her out, all the more because it did not seem to me that she would live to a ripe old age; perhaps I even felt a bit sorry for her. But I continued on my way. I'm not in the mood for making-good-again with any German.

This entire area must have been leveled by Allied bombers and how now been rebuilt. Berlin's modern architecture is really quite awful, and never more so when it makes counter-depressive attempts at livening up its bleak urban environment with random and meaningless slashes of color or unusual forms. And the buildings seem so bulky. Many of them run the entire length of the block, and the stern impression their size conveys is heightened by the fact that so many of the roads they flank are extremely wide.

I looked in at the Kaiser Wilhelm Gedachtniskirche – the Memorial Church, a memorial to Bismark's Kaiser. What remains of the structure represents the worst of Wilhelmine (the Prussian cousin of Victorian) bad taste – indeed, it is more ponderous than its British equivalent, and lacks its wistful, romantic flavor. A bulky, ungraceful, pompous structure, it reminds me of what Oscar Wilde had to say of a new Balliol building (the one where I lived in my first year at Oxford): *c'est magnifique, mais ce n'est pas le gare*! One has to feel grateful that not more of the church survived the Allied bombs. What is left of its façade is spattered with bullet holes. I noticed here, and elsewhere in Berlin, that when these bullet holes are repaired (the work goes on to this day) only a perfunctory attempt is made to match the color of the mortar to that of the surrounding stone, so that the bullet holes are, if anything, even more apparent than they would have been if left unrepaired. A plaque on one wall states that the destruction of the church in an air raid is "a reminder of God's judgment on us during the years of the war". My first inclination was to feel grateful at this apt and unambiguous acknowledgment of Germany's crimes.

However, just a little parsing of the statement made me recognize that it has no substance, and acknowledges no responsibility - it is merely another instance of those sly ambiguities about "those years" that the Germans have become so adept at formulating. It overlooks the fact that the felonies that incurred God's high-explosive wrath surely began six years or so earlier than "the years of the war". Nor does it identify the evil deeds at which God's judgment was directed. And because these are not identified, any passer-by might reasonably suppose that they were not much different from the deeds that caused God's judgment to descend, also in the form of enemy bombs, upon the churches of Britain and other countries. This is by no means the only instance I have come across when Germans try to sneak away from themselves by implying the equivalence of their deeds with those of the Allies.

Today is September 11, and in the new church attached to the destroyed one a prayer service is being held for the victims of that day, and also for the victims of the Katerina hurricane. I wonder why Germans mourn American tragedies. Why don't they also mourn the horrendous toll of about 1000 Shiite pilgrims - a greater number, possibly, than those killed by the hurricane - who were crushed to death on a bridge in Baghdad the other day? I'm afraid that I wonder how unambiguous their grief really is. I suspect that it may please many Germans, and other western Europeans, to view the Katrina debacle as evidence of America's decline (that many of them seem fervently to hope for): and perhaps also of "God's judgment".

I had a heart-warming email from Adam today telling me that I shouldn't feel upset if I achieve nothing on this trip. How could he possibly have known that I dread "failing" on this trip, (even though I still have no idea what would make it either a failure or a success)? And then I had an email from my wife to say that Abigail and *her* Adam had paid a surprise visit. That also was very thoughtful. I am touched, as well as wryly amused, to see that our two younger children are now starting to take care of us! I continue to worry and wonder about why I came here and whether I am up to whatever task it may be that I have set for myself. And I continue to fight against the spontaneous thought that often comes to me that "all this" is so unimaginable that it could not possibly have happened. But I've already confirmed to my own satisfaction that the poisonous waters of the past are flowing not very far below the surface of the reality that is Berlin today.

When I arrived here three days (years?) ago I made a point of looking at Germans who were probably 75 or older (i.e., born no later than 1930). A Google search indicated that there are about six million – that figure! – of them, or about one in every 13 or 14 Germans. On the next two days I tried hard to catch the eye of such people, staring at them in an obvious and rude way – but I never got a rise from any of them. I imagined a dialogue between them and me along these lines: Old Nazi, "Why are you looking so angrily at me?" Me: "How old are you?" ON: "82", Me: "that's why!"

Today however I escalated matters by not only staring hard at such people but silently mouthing a curse upon them. Depending on how one looks at the matter this behavior is childish, ridiculous, or alarming. In any event, I haven't been able to get the slightest response. It seems almost as though people here will do anything to avoid eye contact.

I saw a man today who, from the way he was talking with his companions, seemed to be a humorous, intelligent, altogether affable person; I thought he was probably in his late '30's. When he raised his hand to straighten his hair I saw that a wide and livid scar ran almost the entire length of his forearm, from elbow to wrist. My immediate impulse was to feel sorry for him, but a moment later, as I became aware of my response, I negated it with an inner shrug of indifference.

I don't justify this reaction. I merely record it. I don't think that I would have that reaction to anyone but a German. I've been brought up to believe that hatred is bad. It is morally reprehensible, and psychologically debilitating. We should love our neighbors as ourselves.

But the wall between us and the Germans is redoubtable and precludes neighborly feelings. The Germans built it with hate and it is with hate that we preserve it. I cannot find that I have a right to forgive or overlook what they have done to us; and so I cannot find that I have a right *not* to hate them.

This hatred debases me, I know. It does not bring me pleasure. And it is assuredly not something I cherish for its own sake. But it is the only instrument I know of that enables me to retain a valid, living memory of what happened here, and to be assured that *it really did happen*. This remembering and this knowing - that is what really matters! It matters far more than our civilized reluctance to hate, or the disapprobation that hatred incurs from people who are too good for it.

That it really did happen? Yes, that seems to be a perpetual challenge for me. I can so easily be beguiled - disarmed! - by Berlin's shabby and unattractive banality; it is an effort for me not to see it as an altogether unexceptional place. If I opened my eyes one day and looked around me without knowing where I was, I might well see only its illusion of ordinariness, and not recognize that I was in this benighted place, this horrible, horrible, wicked place, humanity's cesspool, Satan's temple. Is there any other place in the world where there has been so dense a concentration of such evil people? This is the city Hitler lived in. He lived right here! And so did Himmler and Goebbels, and Goering, and Streicher, to name but a few of them. This is the city where the world came to pay obeisance to Hitler in the Olympic Games. This is the city where an accursed bunch of upper-middle level functionaries came together to draw up plans for the efficient fulfillment of their dream of exterminating the Jewish people. On these streets, Jews were beaten and humiliated, were denied entry to shops and restaurants, and were not allowed to travel in busses or sit on park benches. It was from the universities of this city that Jewish students were expelled, books burned and Jewish faculty dismissed, from its hospitals that Jewish doctors and nurses were driven out. It was from the courthouses of this city that Jewish lawyers and judges were barred – anti-Nazi but by no means philo-Semitic Thomas Mann said that he didn't think this was such a big deal – and in them that the legality of the Nuremberg Laws were upheld. It was in this city, too, that work by Jewish artists was removed from museums, and that Jewish musicians were expelled from orchestras. All of this was publicly known but inspired not one single public protest in this iniquitous place. Not one Berliner stood up anywhere and said: this is wrong. Let's not do this. When the plans drawn up by the functionaries of mass murder began to be implemented, the citizens of this hideous city watched in silence as well over 165,000 of their fellows were taken away to be murdered. Not one Berliner, not one, stood up and said, we should not be doing this: please, let these people, the men and women, and all those children, let them live. No one person said that. This Berlin, this ordinary, dull-looking place, was the heart and brains and lungs of the Third Reich. It was from here that a tsunami of mass murder spread out and engulfed all of Europe. It is from this accursed place that obscure towns and villages that we would otherwise never have heard of were transformed into places of unparalleled evil and sadness - Sobibor, Treblinka, Theresienstadt, Auschwitz, Buchenwald, Maidanek, and so many more.

And yet this Berlin is a banal-looking place. It does not *look* evil. The cloaca that is its soul is sealed off, so that it is hard to discover any evidence of its very existence. Florence Miale and I were able to show that the Nazi leaders were anything but banal: but we were able to do so because we had their responses to psychological tests. Here, in Berlin, on the other hand, there is almost no such more or less tangible evidence. All we have to remind us of the reality of this place is memory, and memory if encouraged to do so can change shapes with Proteus for advantage – most recently, in the *diktat* of Chancellor Schroeder that has converted Germany's defeat at the hands of the Allies into Germany's "liberation" from the Nazis.

The tangible evidence of this calamity are the few reluctant monuments (no match they, for the ones that the Germans were *happy* to put up, like the immense Siegesaulle that commemorates various nineteenth-century defeats of the French) and a few streets or plazas named for the involuntarily departed such as Walter Benjamin or Lotte Lenya (the Wagnerplatz however, celebrating the infamous life of Hitler's favorite composer, is far more imposing). *Walter Benjamin*? How many people in Germany have even the slightest idea who he was?!

Today, the memory of the Holocaust is preserved – freeze dried, stuffed by history's taxidermists – in these few monuments and signs, occasional museum exhibitions and a diminishing trickle of books and movies. The survivors are tired of telling their stories; we are tired of hearing them. It won't be all that many years before the last Jew with a number tattooed on his or her arm will be buried.

"Shall we visit the Holocaust Museum today, dear?" and the couple drives off in their shiny BMW to see the new exhibit there. Is that the best we can do for the memory of all those tortured, murdered, souls?

It is not enough that we remember only now and then and without ever *really* remembering, what Amalek did to us.

And why is that not enough? Because the perpetrators are always here, alive, and their victims are always nowhere and dead, their dimming memory encapsulated with a "take as prescribed" or merely a "take when you feel like it".

The victims are entitled to our unending grief. The perpetrators deserve our unending hatred. Either will enable the memory to persist. But grief is hobbled by the limits of our imagination. Who can imagine those final moments in the gas chamber, those naked bodies jammed together, the fear, the disbelief, the child beside you sobbing and bewildered, the total darkness relieved only momentarily when the hatch in the roof is opened so that the Zyklon-B pellets can be thrown into the chamber?

And our grief is also hobbled by the sheer numbers. No one can grieve for six million individual people, and we cannot encapsulate them in a few symbols - an Anne Frank here, a Janusz Korczak there. It was not symbols who were tortured and humiliated and murdered, but millions of individual human beings, to whose individual reality we are blinded because there are so many of them: their memory is insulted, and not served, when we substitute a few collective symbols for all the millions of them. And if we could find in us a measure of grief commensurate with the tragedy – could we really experience it for more than the instant before it engulfed and destroyed us? I don't think so. And why should I add to the undermining of my life by cultivating constant and unbounded grief? Should the Germans continue to have Jewish victims?

On the other hand - I can live with hate. Hatred is immortal and will not be appeased or fade away. And almost anything, no matter how trivial, can incite it – a person, a flag, a car, a song. It can inform my perception of anything that may be labeled "German". Hatred can bind me to the memory of the evil that is an ingrained part of anything German, and remind me, even if only dimly, of the sufferings of the people on whom the Germans poured their evil. It is not grief but hatred that will enable me to see through the veil of banality that covers Berlin soul to Hitler's goose-stepping warriors parading along Unter den Linden. It is not grief but hatred that will enable me to hear the cheers of the Jew-hating mobs of average Germans gathered to watch them; and the screams of the old Jewish couple Schreiber saw being beaten by a horde of very young children: that was here, right here in Berlin! And it is not grief but hatred that will enable me to hear the enthusiastic endorsement of Hitler's policies made from every Protestant and Catholic pulpit in Germany. By keeping hatred alive I will keep faith with the victims. I don't believe there's another way. But it is worth noting the difference between this thought and the Biblical injunction not to forget what Amalek did to us, that focuses our attention on Amalek's deeds rather than on Amalek himself. I don't find this "hate the evil but not the evildoer" soporific persuasive, for the deeds exist only because Amalek perpetrated them. On the other hand, the Biblical injunction seems valuable to me because it posits an essential connection between Amalek's immediate victims and ourselves ("what Amalek did *to you*"), and thereby links us to - and largely defines us by - the appalling continuity of Jewish suffering that, so far at least, culminated in what the Germans did to us during my lifetime. Moreover, the injunction is *to remember* Amalek's deeds. It asks us, in other words, to adopt a particular mental attitude (remembrance) but it does not ask us to undertake any particular action - such as retaliation - against Amalek. We are to remember - that's all! And in turn that requires us to find the best way of remembering. The injunction does not tell us what that way is, though it implies that we are more likely to find it by remembering the deeds and their doers than by grieving for the victims.

Of course, the Germans have every incentive to choose today's realities over yesterday's memories. Who can blame them, after all, if they repackage their past into a few mediocre monuments and a handful of cunningly ambiguous sentiments? But if the Germans have good reason to want to forget the Jews, the Jews surely have every reason to remember the Germans. Jews and Germans don't cohabit well and neither do the realities of Germany's past with the realities of Germany's present. The present, though, usually emerges as the winner. No doubt, that's generally how things should be. But Berlin's present reality has no value for me; I'm not interested in any part of it.

These past few days I've kept it at bay, in among other ways with a daily portion of Goldhagen's book. This is by far the best book on the subject that I have read; it helps one understand Nazism and the Germans much more deeply than our *Nuremberg Mind* (that, to be fair, only looked at one variable). Goldhagen's is a huge intellectual and scholarly achievement that, perhaps ludicrously, was brought to life as a political science PhD dissertation. What a remarkable exception it is to the rule that social science dissertations, if they are ever quoted, are almost invariably quoted only by their authors and supervisors! Goldhagen has his share of critics, to be sure, but nothing I've read has caused me to doubt his basic thesis.

Goldhagen exposes the lie that the Germans murdered because they were ordered to murder, and that they would have been shot if they refused. He establishes that no one in Nazi Germany was compelled to take part in the murder of Jews. Indeed, the murderers were explicitly offered the choice of *not* participating in these crimes, but they almost never chose that option. Indeed, in certain instances when for cynical reasons Himmler ordered his men to stop murdering Jews, they actually disobeyed his orders and continued the slaughter.

That is why Goldhagen calls his book, "Hitler's willing executioners". And "willing" is the least of it. There is no record of a German in the killing fields ever forgoing the opportunity to murder a Jew. Killing Jews was recognized as a good thing to do. Goldhagen reports that the murderers would sometimes invite their wives or girlfriends from Germany to watch them at work – the only recorded objection to this practice being in the case where a woman was pregnant. It was not thought good for an Aryan fetus to be present at an event like this, though the reason for that is not clear. No, killing Jews was considered good work, work to be proud of, even enjoyable work – there were wild drinking parties after a particularly successful day; and approval of it among the German population at large was so widespread that it was not unusual for men to send photographs of their activities home to their friends and family back in Germany – who no doubt smiled complacently as they saw how enthusiastically and capably young Hans was working to bring the Leader's vision of a better, Jew-free world into being. The anti-Semitism of the Germans was intense. Although it was a crime in those days for a German to have sexual relations with Russians, Poles and other subhumans, thousands of Germans were convicted of this practice. It was also a crime to have sexual relations with a Jew. There is no record of even one German being punished for committing such an unspeakable deed. After all, there are some things that not even the most sex-starved Aryan will allow himself to do.

Goldhagen also shows that German anti-Semitism was not a creation of the Nazis but has for centuries been part of German culture and history. (As children in the years immediately after World War 1, my parents encountered appalling, persistent, anti-Semitism, from their teachers as well as from their school mates.) And what Goldhagen has in mind is not the mere disliking of Jews, but the view of them as Satan's spawn (as Martin Luther, that eminently influential German liked to call us) who endanger the very existence of the German people and who must therefore be exterminated. Goldhagen calls it "Eliminationist anti-Semitism". In the Nazi years the determination to exterminate the Jews was so intense and widespread that the Germans were willing to risk losing the war if only they could achieve the destruction of Jewry. Imagine how well they could have fought the Allies if they had not diverted all those resources to the destruction of our people. If they had not driven out all those remarkable Jewish scientists would it not have been they, and not the Americans, who first manufactured nuclear weapons? The Germans ultimately did not care about such considerations. Exterminating the Jews mattered to them more than winning the war.

It is essential to recognize, too, that the Holocaust was not an unanticipatable anomaly in German history. German history cannot be understood without recognizing the extent to which the forces that created the Holocaust were embedded in Germany's past. And the people who advocated, supported, carried out the Holocaust were not just from the fringes of German society. Eliminationist anti-Semitism was the norm in Germany well before Hitler began advocating it (which he did as early as 1921, without particularly scandalizing anyone). As the years advanced a small number of anti-Nazi Germans came, all too discreetly and all too belatedly, to the fore. Yet what is so depressing to realize is that even anti-Nazi Germans – Barth, Niemoller, Thomas Mann, the people who tried to assassinate Hitler in 1944 - were anti-Semitic. They detested the Nazis but – as good Germans – they also detested the Jews.

Not all anti-Semitism is lethal. Much of it is merely unpleasant. But in Germany *all* anti-Semitism, including that of Hitler's opponents, was grist to the wheel of mass extermination. In its least malign form it gave a nod of approval to the people who were directly involved in the murdering, which means that a huge majority of Germans condoned what happened. They supported the murder, they thought it a good idea, they did not oppose it. So that when we talk of German guilt we are indeed talking about the guilt of the Germans, from which only a very small number of good people are immune. That's what my gut tells me. Hatred doesn't draw fine distinctions.

But still, what about today's Germans, most of whom were not even alive during the Nazi era?

Unhesitatingly, I include them among the guilty, among those from whom I recoil in hated, disgust, fear. Dan Rustow was the only certifiably good German I've known. But that's not because all three of his wives were Jews. After all, Thomas Mann's wife was a Jew, too! No, Dan was a profoundly decent man who, on his own, fled from Nazi Germany at the age of 16. Not only because he was an anti-Nazi but because he was not an anti-Semite. Dan was indeed *Dankwart*, and I remember him with affection and respect.

The finding of a recent poll is that about 36% of all Germans are anti-Semitic – thirty-eight percent! That's the largest proportion in all Europe. Larger even than the proportion of anti-Semites in that most traditionally anti-Semitic of all European countries, Poland .

And over 50% say that Jews talk too much about the Holocaust... Now the people willing to expose such attitudes to poll takers are for the most part too young to have acquired them in Nazi Germany.[5] So how *did* they come to hold those attitudes - surely, they were not just acquired a few weeks ago?

Today's German anti-Semites, no matter how young they are, are directly linked to their predecessors, the Nazis. No doubt some Germans recoiled from their anti-Semitism in 1945 when they saw where it had led them. But I don't doubt that after they were "liberated", as their Chancellor Schroeder puts it, most of them carefully folded up their antisemitism and kept it safe and dry in the closet until the time comes when it can be worn again. True, successive German governments have worked to move Germany away from its grim past. Hence, all those monuments, all those programs, hence even the legally-mandated blocking of internet searches that contain such words as "Nazi" or "Hitler". But even without considering the fact that the people who make up the German government are themselves Germans, with all that that implies about how they *really and truly* feel about the Jews, there's only so much a government can do, only so much willingness a government can have to acknowledge frankly its country's shame – and only so much that a government is likely to do (let alone actually *want* to do) when it knows it will not be re-elected if it goes too far out on a limb. And as Schroeder said not so long ago, the

---

[5] The phoniness of much German remorse, even on the part of younger generations, is documented by a German academic's statement – it seems certain that he did not know that it was incriminating – in a scholarly American periodical: "If you are a German in the United States, that *one* subject always comes up quickly, and you are asked politely about it...Many of the Germans I know in the United States have gone through a transformation: they try to act as un-German – as much against the stereotype – as possible. That's not as difficult as it sounds ... you learn to be the 'good German' who is struggling appropriately with his past, the German who is always ready to show feelings of guilt, the German who dislikes any kind of German patriotism..." Peter Schneider, "A Hero with a Blind Spot", *WQ The Wilson Quarterly* (2001), pp.68-69.

time has now come for Germany to stop apologizing for its past (despite that however he did *not* get re-elected!)

And so, the no-longer-to-be-apologized-for past is officially switched off, and Germany can now thank Russia and the three western allies for liberating Germany from the Nazis! Everything has been made good again – *wieder gut gemacht*. Berchtesgaden is once more a lovely place in the Bavarian Alps. Dachau is again a famous center of medieval art.

This is how just about all Germans, and not merely a few elderly veterans of the good old days, the Nazis, restructure their past, and perceive their present reality. And this effective maneuver, one that is however never quite effective enough, for it has to be buttressed over and over again, this manipulating of the truth, tells me that the past remains with these people. Not just their embarrassment, regret, or whatever about the Nazis, but also their considerably less than total estrangement from the Nazi past. 36% of Germans express anti-Semitic sentiments. If someone wants to believe that these sentiments were imported from outer space, well, I guess that that's what they will believe. But to my way of thinking these sentiments are part of the living, pulsing, and only lightly somnolent inheritance today's Germans have from the past. They haven't made it good again. How silly of us to think that they really wanted to! And how silly of us to imagine that they couldn't possibly get away with it:

> *A little while more and the wormhole will close.*
> *Forever.*
> *And the names will cease, the faceless names.*
> *And the living will sail on the waters of Wann,*
> *caressed by breezes.*
> *They will soar in bronze cars to the eagle's high*
> *nest.*

I tell myself that I don't hate an individual who is a German – a Hans here, a Brunhilde there - but I'm not sure that that's true. Does hating the Germans make me feel better? No, of course it doesn't. Why should it? But it does make me feel that I haven't turned away from my obligation to remember what they did. And whom do I mean by "they"? I think that will become very clear to me in the next day or two.

If 36% of Germans are anti-Semitic, does that mean that 64% of them are not? No, it doesn't mean that. There are surely some - many - who know better in these days than to give anti-Semitic responses to a poll-taker. In 1946, a poll conducted by the U.S. occupation forces found that about 50% of Germans are anti-Semitic. Is anyone going to believe that right after World War 2 only half of Germany's population was anti-Semitic? Of course not. Most of the other half knew that this wasn't the time to voice one's true feelings about the hated race, especially not to a pollster employed by the American occupiers. And so it is today, I believe. And there's also this point to be noted: The proportion of people in Germany's population giving anti-Semitic responses *as measured by the polls* fell only 14% between 1945 and 2005. That's a pretty damn depressing statistic!

In some ways I can feel sorry for the Germans today. It's hard to be a German, particularly when you don't quite understand why it is hard to be a German.

What should Germans do to discharge their debt to their victims? I don't know. Frankly, that's not my problem, and I'm not going to waste even a *Planck* length of my life to help them work that out. But I know that *Wiedergutmachung* hasn't done the job.

Day Four

Things got off to a strange start this morning. Outside the railway station two young people held signs identifying themselves as walking-tour guides. One of them had already assembled a sizable group, whose composition seemed to indicate that they were not here for the Jewish tour. The other guide, a pretty young blonde woman, was standing by herself, looking perhaps a little forlorn. I asked her whether she would be guiding the Jewish tour. "Yes I am", she said. "But I'm not Jewish".

"OK" or "whatever", as the children would say. I could have replied, "I am", but there was no point in being confrontational at the very outset and in any case I didn't think of that response until much later. Our guide has a good Jewish name – Hannah – and she said that she is American. However, I think she is in fact a German, because her soft "G" always came out as a "ch", as in "Chairmany". Supporting this assumption were her many references during the tour to the "brutal" Soviet "invasion" of Germany in 1945, that I don't think your average American graduate student doing her MA in art history abroad is likely to make. Although up to today I had avoided getting into an argument with Germans, I did find it impossible not to remind Hannah that in 1945 the Soviets were driving back the Germans who had invaded the Soviet Union. "Oh yes, of course", was her response which, in its slick evasiveness, strengthened my conviction that she is a German. Another way in which Hannah denigrated the former Communist regime was to repeat, quite contemptuously, that they hadn't built a national holocaust memorial in Berlin. She glided with admirable skill over the objection someone – but not I – made that the West Germans hadn't until very recently, either. Germany's holocaust memorial, an awful structure the size of a football field, and designed - of all people! - by an American Jew, Peter Eisenmann, was opened just a few months ago.

I overheard Hannah talking with a middle-aged American woman in our group who was (as she told me) a convert to Judaism. Hannah's remarks went something like this: "A friend of mine went to her parents' house for dinner the other day, and her favorite uncle was there; and the conversation got round to discussing the war, and it turned out that the favorite uncle had been a concentration camp guard. Can you imagine how difficult it must be to learn that about someone you love?" Hannah's remarks seemed to have something of the "my best friend has become pregnant" circumlocution, and I suspected that she was talking about herself. Poor Hannah! She's a German masquerading as an American while guiding Jews on a tour through Berlin. I felt sorry for her.

A 15-minute ride on the U-Bahn brought us to what had been the Jewish quarter - now a mostly (and expensively) gentrified and of course *Judenrein* neighborhood: a well-set dinner table of a place at which elegant ladies and gentlemen pay no attention to the mummified corpses sitting with them.

I suppose that parts of this area bore some resemblance to the scenes in my Nazi dreams - dark, old buildings, winding streets, cobblestones - but not to the extent that I could say - *that's the building!* Or *that's the street!* Oh well...

Our first stop was on the Rosenstrasse, where we saw the ruins of a synagogue, and a building that Hannah told us had been the synagogue's community center. Early one wintry morning in February, 1943, as part of their final sweep of Jews in Germany who had escaped arrest, the Gestapo rounded up about two thousand Jewish men who were married to Aryan women. The Jews were held in the community center building here on Rosenstrasse, to be transported to the gas chambers as soon as a train became available.

Later that day, however, one or two of the Aryan wives turned up outside the building to demand the release of their husbands. Each day they were joined by more Aryan wives of the Jewish prisoners, and ultimately, it is said, there were about six hundred of them standing silently with their placards outside the community center. And what did the Gestapo do to these women? Did it arrest them? Set dogs on them? Shoot them dead in the street? Haul them off to concentration camps? No. In the end the Gestapo simply gave in. The Jewish husbands were freed.

I did not agree with our guide, Hannah, that this episode shows how decent the average German was during those years. In my opinion, rather, it shows that in at least this one instance the Nazis yielded to a demand that conflicted with their programs and purposes and that the Nazis did not punish (let alone imprison, torture, execute) the people who made this demand, for all that they did so publicly and explicitly. But the Rosenstrasse demonstrations do not tell us anything about the average German. They were the only instance (as far as I know) of Aryans protesting the Final Solution. Naturally, one can't help but wonder how differently things would have turned out if such protests had taken place in towns and villages across Germany. And it must be said, I hope without taking anything away from these very brave women, that they did not act to protect the lives of Jews, as such, but to secure the release of their husbands. I also note the troubling arithmetic of this episode: two thousand Jewish men had been arrested, yet only about six hundred women appear to have participated in these demonstrations. Where were the other fourteen hundred wives?[6] Besporting themselves with their Siegfrieds and Adolfs, no doubt...

---

[6] Back in the hotel Google found for me a book about this episode - *Resistance of the Heart* by Nathan Stoltzfus. Written by a Jew – too bad. This episode is of course something the Germans themselves don't want to celebrate, for it calls attention to the despicable culpability of just about *all* Germans who did not lift a finger to save the Jews.

A short while later we were in a dank and unlovely alleyway reading a plaque on the wall of what had once been a small factory where deaf and blind people made brushes and brooms. The manager of this factory was an Aryan called Otto Weidt, and most of his workers were Jews. Weidt went to great lengths to protect them, and he also hid a number of other Jews who came to him for protection. When a Jewish girl whom he had been harboring was seized by the Gestapo and shipped off to Auschwitz, Weidt actually went there and succeeded in saving her. What a fine, fine man – and what a rare man – Otto Weidt must have been!

And again one can't help wondering why there weren't more people like him. Yad Vashem, the Israeli holocaust memorial organization, has compiled a list of people - it calls them Righteous Gentiles - who tried to save Jews during the war. There are a mere 410 Germans on this list. This is rather less than one-tenth of the number of Righteous Gentiles whom Yad Vashem has identified in notoriously anti-Semitic Poland.

By their actions, the Rosenstrasse wives and Otto Weidt refute the claim that ordinary German people could have done nothing to oppose the Holocaust and save Jewish lives. We always knew that they should have. Now we know that they could have, and that in doing so they would probably not have incurred much danger to themselves, and that they would probably have succeeded in saving millions of lives. But they preferred not to.

Our guide Hannah called our attention to small brass plaques (perhaps 4 inches square) embedded in the cobblestone sidewalk outside some apartment buildings. They are the project of a local conceptual artist, who calls them "stumbling blocks" (I don't remember how one says that in German). Each plaque names a Jew who had lived in the building bordering the sidewalk, his or her date of birth, the concentration camp to which he or she was taken, and the date on which he or she was *"ermoerdert"* – murdered. This is close to the kind of project I had wanted the German government to undertake in my "Jewish landmarks in Germany" project, the differences being (1) that I never got the project off the ground, and (2) that I had not thought of recording the existence of obscure individuals, which is what the "stumbling blocks" do. We went past the site of a bombed-out building (with a café on what is now a lawn); on either side of it are four- or five-storied apartment buildings. The walls of these buildings that face the bombed-out lot have been neatly plastered over, and on what would have been each landing are painted the names of Jews who once had lived in an apartment leading to it. The inscriptions were a little too far away for me to read clearly.

I wonder what these evocations of the murdered Jews convey: what memory there is in them. Four "stumbling blocks" are clustered together. They tell me that Georg Salinger was born in 1892 and his wife Rosa, nee Ginsberg, in 1893; that their daughter Ursula was born in 1919, and their son Gerd in 1922; that Ursula was murdered in Riga in 1942 – she was 23 or 24 years old, and that her brother, barely 20 years old, and her parents were murdered in Auschwitz the following year. I am not entirely inured to these data. They make me feel sad. I find it perplexing that Ursula was murdered in Latvia's capital. I note that Georg and Rosa gave their children good German names, which of course availed them nothing. But neither the information on the plaques nor whatever subtext I can find in it evoke discernible human beings. They memorialize Salingers only in a trivial sense. My response to them would be no different if the murdered people had other names, if they were born in different years, or if they were murdered in different concentration camps. At the very most, the plaques make us recognize that we can never see the dead as real human beings, and that their fate is unimaginable to us. The Salingers, and all the others, and everything that they lived through, have been reduced to 4-inch square brass plaques. Possibly this is precisely the point that the artist wanted to convey.

Very occasionally – particularly in photographs – one *does* recognize an actual human being among those millions of dead Jews. There's that precious little boy in the Warsaw Ghetto holding his hands up high, part of a group of Jews being marched down a street by armed and steel-helmeted German soldiers. There is sheer terror on his face. He has seen appalling things and he knows that even worse awaits him. One wants so desperately to embrace him, and reassure him, and protect him: and these impulses establish that we are in the presence of an actual human being. This is one of the most terrible photographs ever taken. It reminds us momentarily that it was millions of real men, real women and real children whom the Germans murdered.

Even in these very rare instances, however, our own good fortune makes it impossible to know the reality of what these murdered Jews experienced. We are strangers to the smells, the sounds, the colors of mass murder; we cannot know the tensions that grip the body of a person who is about to be murdered; we can't know the terror, the hunger and thirst, the feeling of despair and abandonment, the cleverly-contrived humiliations, the beatings, and other indignities and agonies – as for instance being forced to lie down (naked of course) in an open pit on the bodies (naked of course) of Jews who've already been shot, while you wait for the bullet that will shatter your skull, too.

Really, I don't think that we can remember the victims in any way that does them justice. We can only retain the knowledge that millions of people were killed, usually with a great deal of sadistic ingenuity (showers!) merely because they were Jews. There is no memory worth having in the fact that a Jew named so-and-so lived in this building or in the fact that he was killed – murdered, I should say – in such and such a place and on such and such a date. And the few whom we do see as persons, whom we can imagine ourselves speaking to, and comforting, and hoping to protect, like that little boy in the Warsaw Ghetto, if we are to remember them as real people we cannot use them as symbols of all the forgotten others.

We cannot know the six million victims and we cannot mourn for people who are, at best, dim shadows. But there is very much that we do know about the men and women who murdered them. We have detailed biographies of many of them, even psychological profiles. We know how their actions were organized, we have detailed knowledge of the problems they encountered as they went about their murdering, and the solutions they found to those problems. We know how they accounted for their miserable lives to interrogators after the war. We have photographs of them hard at work murdering Jews. And all this detailed information enables us to know them and what they did far more vividly than we can ever know their victims, who came from every walk of life, were religious or unreligious, were good people or bad people, were of every age, and spoke a dozen different languages - and who now exist, with rare exceptions, only as one line in a seemingly interminable list of the names of murdered Jews. We cannot feel passionate grief about people whom we never knew, and of whom there are so few, and such superficial, reminders.

I think I can only discharge my obligation to the murdered ones by focusing my attention on their murderers.

Instead of grief there is hatred.

Most people, most Jews certainly, have learned to think of the Holocaust as a unique event, a categorically unprecedented event. But that is not correct. The Passover ritual includes the words, *bchol dor vador 'omdim 'aleinu lechaloteinu* - in every generation they rise up against us to destroy us - and if we believe that to be actually or mythically true then we cannot believe that the Holocaust is unprecedented in Jewish history. Not to mention the innumerable instances of genocide elsewhere in the human family - most of which, in all likelihood, were so complete that we have no record of them. And not to mention, too, that among the earliest genocides of which we possess records are those - chronicled in the books of Judges and Joshua - that were perpetrated by our own ancestors.

Is it more reprehensible to murder a person because he belongs to a particular group than to murder him for any other reason? The answer is that in a very specific sense it *is* worse, because in the former instance the murder is likely to be only one of many (the other members of the group) that have been or will be committed, whereas in the latter instance additional murders are not necessarily indicated. However, that is not the same as saying that murdering Jews or attempting to exterminate the entire Jewish people is worse than murdering members of some other group or attempting to exterminate the entire group. But where does this leave me as a Jew? Certainly, the horror and wickedness of the Holocaust is not intensified by arguing that the event was unique, nor diminished by the argument that it was not. Candidly, I don't know what distinguishes the Holocaust from other mass murders except the scale of it. (But don't historians think that Stalin probably had many millions of kulaks murdered? And would it matter, from a moral standpoint, if he only had one million of them slaughtered?) To my mind at least the Holocaust matters very particularly because it involved the destruction of my own people. But I also see it as exemplifying or reminding us of the destruction of so many other peoples. There's a touchy-feely old *midrash* that says something to this effect: all suffering that is Israel's (i.e., the Jews') alone is not suffering. All suffering that Israel shares with others is suffering. There's some truth and much ethical value to this. But when all is said and done I feel the destruction of my own people far more intensely than the destruction of other peoples. And I suppose that that may be part of the reason why other people – Gentiles – don't care as much about the Holocaust as we do.

The next stop on our tour was at a large and somewhat overgrown plot of land. Only the memorial plaque on a wall and a single gravestone indicated that this had been a Jewish cemetery. Indeed, it is the oldest Jewish cemetery in Berlin. Yet, it is not a graveyard, because the Germans leveled it and there are no graves here any longer. Moreover, that single gravestone is a fake. It purports to be the resting place of Moses Mendelssohn, and stones and other remembrances on and around the headstone show that there are people who believe that it is. But the fact is that the Germans destroyed the entire cemetery and did not leave a single stone in place, so that there is no real way of telling who is buried where - if indeed the corpses and skeletons were not disinterred, as they may well have been, by the Germans. Moreover, the *soi disant* Mendelssohn headstone is obviously a new one. It can't have been put up more than thirty or forty years ago, at the latest. It is another example, and by no means an innocuous one, of the prettying up of history in which the Germans indulge themselves.

I remembered here the last time I stood in a Jewish graveyard in Germany. Back in the early '80s I'd been trying to get German foundations and the German government to create a catalog of Jewish sites in the federal republic. This led to my being invited to a scholarly conference in Wolfenbuettel, Lessing's home town, on the subject of Jewish graveyards in Germany. The conference was funded by the Volkswagen Foundation, the making-good-again organ of an organization that has a lot to make good again, and it was this foundation that paid for my travel expenses.

The conference, predictably enough, was dull and uninteresting. On its last day the mayor of Wolfenbuettel came along with us to visit the local Jewish cemetery. It proved to be an old and tired-looking place without any allure whatsoever. Gravestones were tilting at odd angles; the grass had obviously not been cut for a while; paint on the few benches there was crackled. But the overall feeling of the place was bland and not disagreeable – after all, no one had mourned anyone here for more than four decades, and (untypically) the cemetery had not been visited by vandalizing anti-Semites. I could have stayed for a long while in this place, musing about many things. The mayor however made a speech, various professors and other functionaries had their say, and now there was a pause, with no one evidently quite sure what was to come next. I raised my hand. "This graveyard", I said, "looks quite neglected, and perhaps that is not inappropriate, given the circumstances." I then pointed to one area in the compound that looked entirely different. "But over there, why, the place is immaculate. It reminds me of our Arlington National Cemetery in Washington D.C., where everything is freshly painted, the grass is immaculately trimmed –

an entirely orderly place. Perhaps someone could tell me about this area."

At first no one spoke. Then the mayor stepped forward and, with the oft-practiced matter-of-fact smoothness Germans will have when referring to those years, he explained. The federal government provides the town of Wolfenbuettel every year with a certain amount of money for each Jewish grave, but this is enough to provide only minimal care and maintenance. The other part of the cemetery is where Russian prisoners-of-war were buried. (Evidently, Russians and Jews deserved no better than to be buried in each others' company.) In the 1950's Germany and the Soviet Union signed a pact that set certain standards for the upkeep of graveyards in which each other's prisoners of war were buried. Under the terms of this pact, the German government allocates a certain amount for the care and maintenance of Soviet prisoners' graves in Germany. This amount is approximately 15 times greater than the same government allocates for the care and maintenance of Jewish graves. Hence the very obvious difference between the two parts of the graveyard in which we were now standing.

I looked around our little cluster of necrophiliac scholars. None seemed at all uncomfortable with these facts. And that was when I decided to abandon my landmarks project. I just didn't want to have anything more to do with Germans. I just couldn't see myself ever returning to this horrid country.

The Israeli couple on our Jewish walking tour had a linen shopping bag on which were printed the German flag and a picture of the Bundestag, (as it was designated in this instance). I couldn't quite understand what status or identity or whatever Israelis might hope to get with a bag like that. Would "yes, we just returned from a week in Germany!" boost their prestige back home in Tel Aviv?

At the last part of our walking tour we were taken to see what is called The Big Synagogue – what an architectural horror! It was destroyed by the Nazis and now gives the impression of having been restored to its former gaudiness. Yet it isn't a building at all, in any conventional sense, but a Potemkin façade, behind which is only a narrow hallway containing some dull historical exhibits about the synagogue. Beyond that there is an empty lot, the land on which the main part of the synagogue had once stood. What apt symbolism! A flashy façade conveys an impression of modern-day Germany's benevolence toward the Jews. But it is merely a façade, a structure without substance or life that mocks itself and those responsible for it.

At the end of our tour our guide, Hannah, having dwelt on Russian "brutality" during what she calls "the invasion" of Berlin, and on the failure of the DDR to restore Berlin, build monuments, etc., now narrates in great detail the sorry story of the ship St Louis, the thrust of which of course is that the countries that wouldn't admit the Jewish refugees from Germany were also responsible for their deaths. She's right of course, and as a Jew I cannot regard FDR, who was responsible for the decision to turn the ship back, with anything less than detestation. But I don't think that this was an appropriate point for our guide to make, under the circumstances.

Day Five

It seems that of several hundred thousand German soldiers captured by the Russians only about ten thousand lived to return to the *Vaterland*. I watched a documentary about them on the television set in my hotel room. The film opened with the camera panning slowly over the despairing faces of women on a station platform as they realized that their menfolk were not among the small group of repatriated prisoners on the train that had just arrived from Russia. Spontaneously, instinctively, I felt for those poor women; but I soon recognized how misplaced my sympathy for them was. The tragedy after all is not that almost all the captured Nazi soldiers died but that they and their fellows invaded Russia, devastated its economy, and murdered as many as fifteen million Russian civilians. It seems to me that Germans who get all teary about the suffering of their men on the Russian front might do well to ask why those men went there in the first place, and what they did once they were there. It would have been more appropriate for the German filmmakers to focus on that than on the self-pity of the defeated aggressors. I see no reason to mourn for the who died in Soviet hands. They were murdering brutes. They sowed the wind and they reaped the whirlwind.

No: that's not correct, for the "wind" the Germans sowed was far more devastating than the "whirlwind" they reaped.[7]

The next evening I watched another documentary, this time about the suffering of German soldiers in the Battle of Stalingrad, though it also had a couple of brief Jew-slaying scenes (one of which I am certain never to forget) for balance. It was easy to forget, while

---

[7] A 1965 German Red Cross study estimated German civilian deaths at the hands of the Red Army at about 500,000. That's about one-*thirtieth* of the Russian civilians killed by the Germans.

watching this film, that it was in fact the Germans who had attacked the city, and that the reason they were eventually encircled and killed by Soviet troops was because Hitler had ordered them not to retreat or surrender. At least 25,000 Russian civilians were killed by the Germans during merely the first week of the battle – no one knows how many more died in the five months during which the fighting raged – and, again, it struck me as outrageous that the film I was watching should have focused on the suffering of the German invaders.

I remember now an old German woman who was my fellow passenger on the train to Wolfenbuettel several years ago. I don't know *how* old she was, but she was certainly an adult for at least part of "those years". She had been visiting some relatives in Hannover, she told me, and now was returning to her home in East Germany. It seems that the East German regime had no objection to elderly people crossing the border into the West and, as far as it was concerned, they could remain there if they chose to. In any event, this woman went on and on in her thick peasant accent, which I could barely understand, about how hard life was, and how much she was suffering under the communist regime, and she worked herself up to such a point that tears were rolling down her cheeks as we neared Wolfenbuettel. I didn't have the heart to tell her that her sufferings and the sufferings of her fellow East Germans were nothing compared to the sufferings that they had caused the Jewish – and other – people. And that she and all Germans had brought these sufferings upon themselves. And that they deserved them, and much more, besides.

This evening I have been watching another documentary, this one about Kemal Attaturk. I hadn't realized that he died as recently as 1938, or that it was he who ended the Caliphate (I had assumed that it was the British who did that). The documentary dwelt largely on the Armenian massacres, on Kemal's totalitarian style, and on his admiration of Hitler and Mussolini. The subtext here for a German audience is: we weren't the only shits.

Perhaps not. But you were the worst. By far.

Some of Goldhagen's critics have argued that anti-Semitism during the Hitler years could not have been as intense and widespread as he claimed because if it had been it would be far more prevalent in Germany today – an unexpected setting, this, for the *post hoc ergo propter hoc* fallacy. Part of Goldberg's rebuttal is that the generally positive state of racial/ethnic relations in the U.S. today can hardly be taken to mean that there has always been little or no racism in America. A curious way, I think, of responding to a very flaccid attack on his thesis.

The starting point of apologists' critique, of course, is totally false. Anti-Semitism *is* alive and well in Germany today. 36% of its population gives anti-Semitic responses in polls, and 50% say that Jews talk too much about the Holocaust. I think that this is an astonishingly high level of toxicity. In fact, it is the highest in western Europe. And of course it is only the crassest people who will acknowledge their anti-Semitism to an interviewer. Many others will be too well-bred to disclose their true feelings. (I am reminded of the inscription I once saw on a German "memorial" that denounced anti-Semitism as "a lack self-control", the message being that Jew-hatred is understandable but that one should not express it!)

Goldhagen took a great deal of heat from his critics, more perhaps than he, as a very young man, knew how to handle. On at least one occasion he even went so far as to suggest – almost as if he were pandering - that German history is no longer on its *Sonderweg*, on its distinctive path. That is not a point of view I would care to endorse. At the very least, it is premature.

But of course, we don't need to look at Germany today to recognize that Germany yesterday was virulently, murderously and totally anti-Semitic.

Indeed, I don't know how valid another part of Goldhagen's rebuttal is. Race relations in America today may be rather less positive than they appear to be. The appalling scenes from New Orleans in the wake of Katrina these past few weeks suggest that a great deal of racism remains – even if it is not always visible to most of us – in American society. It will be instructive to see how long it takes for today's intense concern about the poor, aka the Blacks, in New Orleans to drift away into indifference, and for today's enormous flow of material aid to dry up. (I'm curious to know, too, how much of that aid actually reaches the people who need it.)

For that matter, I don't know why people believe that today's Germany *could be* fundamentally different from yesterday's. I don't think that ideas and attitudes are readily discarded (even if they seem to be discredited) from one generation to the next. The very great majority of Germans before 1945 openly believed that the Jews posed an imminent threat to the well-being and even to the survival of the German people. They did not think of us as an inferior race, like the Slavs or Blacks, but as the fantastically potent spawn of the Devil. We were so toxic, the Germans believed, that even a person who had only one Jewish parent – a quarter-Jew – carried the lethal poison with him or her. In facing this danger half-measures would not suffice. Only the extermination of every Jew could save the German people. German anti-Semitism, in other words, was not mere dislike or hatred of Jews. It was in Goldhagen's phrase, *exterminationist*. These views were freely and forcefully expressed by every influential person in Germany and were a basic tenet of the German polity during the Hitler years.

Can we believe that this intense and deeply-rooted murderous hatred of the Jews disappeared from one day to the next with the defeat of the Nazis in May 1945? Including from the hearts and minds of little children whose parents and teachers had planted it in their souls?

And here's a related point. I am thinking of my paternal grandparents, who were very, very religious. Their son, my father, was demonstratively un-religious but then became observant again, albeit in the Reform/Liberal mode. (In fact, even when he was in his anti-religious mode he was a committed freemason, which is itself a form of religiosity, and he apparently enjoyed the many Jewish associations in its ceremonies.) In the third generation, I have been religious at certain times and in some respects have admired and even envied the orthodox, but I now have very negative feelings about religion and religiosity and don't understand how I could ever have taken them seriously. Despite this, all four of my children give Judaism more than a passing nod and I will be the only one in my family who does not mark Rosh Hashanah this year. All of this shows that convictions, ideologies, beliefs, are not that easily eradicated, even when it seems that history has passed them by...

The time may come when there is a generation of Germans who have no feelings, one way or another, about the Jews. But until that time the heritage of anti-Semitism will be passed on from one generation of Germans to the next.

The children and grandchildren of the murderers have inherited the lies and rationalizations that they now use to gloss over their deeds. ("He didn't know until after the war"; "he was always an anti-Nazi, of course"; "he was only in the Waffen-SS" – and so on.) I daresay that their organization of reality is also one that they inherited from their elders: as when they refer to the "barbaric" Soviet "invasion" of Germany. Are we to believe that when the younger generations learned these equivocations they did not also acquire the hatred and ideological fervor that those equivocations are intended to mask? I don't think so!

The anti-Semitic fervor of their parents and grandparents was the cauldron in which the anti-Semitism of today's younger Germans was brewed. I therefore consider it permissible and perhaps even prudent to include younger Germans in my anathema. And this despite all the window dressing one sees everywhere in Berlin. I'm writing this in a restaurant in Walter-Benjaminplatz. Score one for making-it-good-again. But I'm also mindful of the fact that, just a few blocks away, and much bigger, is the Richard-Wagnerplatz. Score two for the good old days. And that's the way things are here.

When I was in Germany working on my Dachau book, I learned that the compound where the SS personnel who ran the camp lived now houses some Special Forces units of the German army, or perhaps it is of the Bavarian police. It is therefore closed to the general public, and the entrances to it are guarded by armed soldiers. Which only made me want to see inside the compound that much more. I spoke to the unit's commanding officer from a phone in a guardhouse, and told him that my book on Dachau would not be complete without a glimpse of the quarters today. He agreed to let me in and sent a young officer to show me around. This young officer proved to be a rather surly person, clearly displeased with his assignment, and he drove me around at breakneck speed in a Jeep-like German vehicle, but not so fast that I was unable to get a clear picture of the compound. The entire area looked like an elegant and expensive resort. Impressive villas were set on spacious and well-tended lawns; there were fine trees and beds of flowers everywhere; and even the apartment buildings where (I assume) the non-commissioned ranks of the prison staff had been housed were freshly painted and obviously in very good condition. I couldn't help fixating on the massive German eagles that topped the archways into those apartment buildings, and one that was on top of a sort of triumphal arch under which we passed on our hurried tour, because each and every one of those German eagles clutched a swastika in its talons, and what was especially remarkable was that the eagles and the swastikas were freshly painted and in perfect condition. I asked my young German lieutenant about them. "*Ach so!*" he replied, "it is very difficult to get rid of them, you see, they are made of very heavy concrete!"

The sentiments that those swastikas express are also (I believe) very difficult to get rid of.

I am sitting at a sidewalk table of the Café Kampinski on the corner of Fesanenstrasse and Kurfurstendamm. The coffee here is good. But my main purpose in being here is to take photographs of the older people walking by, this being one of the more crowded parts of the town. The shutter release on my little digital camera takes an unusually long time to work, and I couldn't catch some of the people who were alive and well in the good old days; many of the other photographs are too blurred to be of any value to me. But that doesn't matter all that much because part of this exercise is to be entirely overt about taking these people's pictures. I want them to know that my camera is pointing at them. I hope that it makes them uncomfortable - but good lord, how comfortable they do look: comfortable, complacent (after all, they've gotten away with it!) , well-dressed, well-fed. I'm hoping that one of them may demand to know why I'm taking their photograph, but that hasn't happened. Looking (on the camera's screen) at some of the better photographs I'm struck by their resemblance to pictures one used to see of Nazis on the run - slightly blurred, taken through a telephoto lens, but with a menacing yet furtive look on their faces.

No sooner do I make this point to myself, however, than I ask myself again: Is it reasonable to regard all Germans as guilty? Or even all Germans of a certain age? My immediate answer is that it is wrong to do so. But in my heart of hearts I know that it is not.

There is an additional context to my thinking about the Holocaust right now that has nothing to do with Germany and the

Germans. Just the other day the president of the United States, reeling from public criticism of his administration's incompetence in coping with the Katerina catastrophe, said that he doesn't know whether his government has the ability to cope with the aftermath of a major terrorist attack – and this four years after 9/11 and the expenditure of who knows how many hundreds of billions of dollars! Here in Europe one gets the impression from reading the papers that America is still viewed as *allmaechtig* – all powerful – and competent, but this view seems to me to be increasingly at odds with the reality of America today. The objective dangers we face are (in my view) enormous, but we have entrusted our defense against them to a government run by religious fanatics, incompetents, and George Bush's former roommates. I had supported Bush because of the decisiveness and clarity of vision he showed in the aftermath of 9/11; but those strengths are less apparent now and they seem to matter less than before as it becomes clearer how flawed, ineffective and unaccountable Bush and the people he works with really are. And this is not only in terms of the terrorist threat, and Iraq. World health officials are warning of a devastating pandemic - the avian flu. Enormous (and growing) budgetary and balance-of-payments deficits are going to cause us major economic problems. Our military is equipped (barely!) for a war it is not fighting; our intelligence capabilities are less than impressive; and our prestige in the international arena is declining precipitously. To top if all off, Bush's ineptitude is challenged by an opposition that seems equally inept. The Democrats have no vision; their strategy is apparently to do nothing and let the Republicans destroy themselves. Which no doubt they will do.

And what I'm leading up to with all this is that our peril – as Jews, I'm thinking now: but of course also our peril as Americans – will increase as America weakens. Racism, generally, and anti-Semitism, are more or less somnolent just now, but instances are not hard to find. And in a prolonged crisis they could emerge with great viciousness. The connection between these apprehensions and my musings about the Germans is not direct except in the sense that I'm more aware than ever, now – here in Berlin – of the terrible forces that are dormant in every society, and sleep only lightly. It doesn't take much to awaken them. And Germany is an extreme example of what can happen when they do awake.

I am lunching in the restaurant of the Jewish community center on Fasanenstrasse. All that is left of the original building (destroyed by the Nazis, it hardly seems necessary to say), is a small portion of the main doorway. There is a heavy police presence both outside the building and at the entrance to it. Almost everyone here appears to be from Russia, and most of them are elderly, certainly much older than I. Russian and Yiddish songs are played over loudspeakers in the restaurant, and the menu offers mainly East European Jewish food like *tschulent, parogy, latkes*: not my favorite cuisine, and not particularly well done, it would seem, even by its own not very ambitious standards. I'd been expecting something along the lines of a soup kitchen but in fact, the food is surprisingly expensive: possibly this is because it is all *glatt* kosher. It is prepared and served by a staff of Germans who outnumber the people eating here by at least two to one. The great and unmodulated geniality of the two waitresses is so uncharacteristic of the people here in Berlin that I can't help wondering how they really perceive their decrepit Jewish customers. Not that there are many of them. I don't think that even a dozen diners were here during my long and leisurely lunch. Indeed, this entire community center is almost empty, which is just as well. It is not pleasing to think that any Jews live here. But apparently over one hundred thousand of them do. Among them are, if I remember correctly, Daniel Barenboim, the pro-Palestinian Israeli musician who fought to have Wagner performed in Israel, and W. Michael Blumenthal, who came to the United States as a young refugee from Germany and was Secretary of the Treasury during Jimmy Carter's presidency. He now heads the Jewish Museum in Berlin.

Still in the Jewish community center: the library has perhaps 20,000 books, and seems to be run by professional librarians. The lending slips on the rear pastedowns of books I picked out at random showed that many books had never been borrowed and others that had not been borrowed for at least ten years; I found none that had been borrowed in the past 12 months. My own first book had been taken out 7 times, most recently in December, 1984 – over 20 years ago!. I wrote a little note on a rear blank page of it, saying that I wish now that I had written the book in a kinder and more understanding way, and then signed and dated my unauthorized annotation: in the more or less complete confidence that no one will ever read it.

Here in the library I came across a book that lists the Jews from Berlin who were killed by the Nazis: just their names, the district of Berlin in which they lived, and the place and date of their deaths at the hands of the Nazis. The book is enormous. The introduction records, very precisely, that the number of Jews from Berlin who were murdered is 160,564. "*Ihre Namen moegen nie vergessen warden*" it says in the foreword: Their names must never be forgotten. Right. But who now remembers them?

Among these names are Selzers, Spiegels (my paternal grandmother's family name) and Neumanns (my mother's maiden name):

- ADOLF SELZER born in Zastavie, Galicia, in 1893; killed Sachsenhausen 5/28/42;
- BRIGITTE SELZER, born 1/30/1936 in Berlin (what could her parents have been thinking of?) and transported to Auschwitz on 6/19/1942 along with her brother Manfred (b.1932) and mother Fanny (b.1910) The date of their death is unknown. Brigitte would have been 6; her brother 10; their

mother, 32.

- OTTO SELZER, b.1919, deported 9/6/43 to Auschwitz, *"Schicksal ungeklaert"* - - fate unknown. Which is untrue. We know that he was murdered, even though there's no record that shows that he was.

- HERMANN SPIEGEL born in Erdobenye, Hungary, gassed in Lodz in 1942. He may have been from the Hungarian side of our family. (Same first name as my father.)

Among the people with names from my mother's side of the family, the Neumanns. Two are 2 Reginas (this was my grandmother's name), 2 Kaethes, (my mother's name), 2 Kurts, and 1 Ernst (the names of my mother's brothers.)

In the introduction to this gruesome book, a Berlin official refers to his fellow-Germans as *das Volk der Taeter* – the people of the deed-doers, or: the people of those who did it. I think that's an excellent formulation. Every German yesterday, today, and tomorrow belongs to *das Volk der Taeter*.

There is a fine quotation from one of Celan's poems at the beginning of the book - he says of the dead Jews that they have only *ein Grab in den Luften* - a grave in the air.

Also in the library is a 2-volume *Gedenkbuch 1986* that lists the names of all murdered Jews who had lived on what, when the book was published, was the territory of the Bundesrepublik. The introduction by German President Richard Weiszaeker – actually, the text of a speech he made in Israel (did he sing this tune in Germany, too? If so, why wasn't *that* chosen for this book?) – has the unchallengeable statement that *Der Holocaust is ein Eregnis in den Geschichte, dass die Identitaet der Juden und der Deutschen in ihrem Kern beinflusst hat und immer beinflussen wird* - "The Holocaust is an historical event that has influenced and will always influence the core of the identities of the Jews and the Germans". He also says, however, *Schuld ist, wie Unschuhld, persoenlich. Schuld oder Unschuld eines ganzen Volkes gibt es nicht. Aber jeden Deutsche traegt die Erbschaft der Geschichte seines Volkes* - "Guilt like innocence is personal. There is no such thing as the guilt or innocence of an entire nation. But every German is heir to the history of his nation."

But an easy syllogism refutes Weizsaecker's argument that there is no such thing as collective guilt. If every German is heir to his nation's history; and if the murder of six million Jews "will always" be a part of that history, then surely Germany's guilt for the Holocaust is part of the inheritance of every German person. Therefore there is such a thing as collective guilt. QED!

Yet we live in a civilization that is increasingly indifferent to history, and ignorant of it. Naturally, the Germans have a particular incentive to hide themselves from their history. As long as they know something of it they will be forced to recognize the Holocaust, or forced to deny it. But for how many more years will history remain an anchor of people's reality? Not just in Germany, but everywhere else in the western world? Ironically, an awareness of history is more acute nowadays in the Islamic world, which is being agitated by eschatological fantasies of restoring the Caliphate, for goodness sake, and reducing everyone who is not a Muslim to the status of *dhimmi* with rights inferior to those of Muslims. In our part of the world, however, historical awareness is rapidly fading. I am struck by how common it is for people to walk into our bookshop and say that they've a few "very old" books for sale - which turn out to have been published in the 1930's! And I wonder, in particular, what kind of Jewishness can exist if Jews detach themselves from their history. The whole theme of suffering and redemption in Judaism exists only in a historical context. There's abundant evidence to show that Jews in the Holocaust understood their suffering in that context, and believed that it united them with Jews in previous generations who also underwent terrible suffering; a large part of the Jewish liturgy is also rooted in historical memory. I really can't imagine what a person who is unaware of our history would mean when he referred to himself as a Jew! Is it possible, however, that in an a-historical world people will forget that Jews are to be reviled and tormented, and ultimately killed? The sentence upon us is, for sure, one that history carries with it. So perhaps, as we move further and further away from intimacy with history the chapter on Jewish suffering will finally close... And with it, of course, the chapter on German guilt, too.

Yet... let's not overlook Islam's penetration, now purposeful, of the west, at present the European west. The descendants of Poitiers and Vienna, the now suddenly bashful heirs of the Crusaders, have opened Europe's gates: not to go out of them to new glory - Jerusalem redeemed, the Suez canalled - but to let in the sons of Ishmael for the brief and illusory convenience of cheap labor. And Islam's warriors are not so besotted with ignorance and turgid certainty that they are oblivious to the opportunity that the gates, so unthinkingly opened, now offer them. And they see that it is from within that

> *... the dream that can never die -*
> *Spain recovered and dar ul-Islam regnant in Europe:*
> *Of hateful sharia on the banks of the Rhine*
> *Of women shrouded, though alive,*
> *On Rome's Condotti road;*
> *Of reason and atheism*
> *And doubt*
> *Driven from the great universities,*
> *Of imbibers lashed*
> *Of adulteresses stoned*
> *Of public executions,*
> *Of thieves meekly offering their hands*
> *To be severed.*
> *A Europe of cliterectomies*
> *A Europe of silent concert halls*
> *And shuttered laboratories*

> *And uprooted vineyards*
> *Ruled by nasty old men*
> *Answerable only to Allah*

And Islam's dreams of world conquest have a particular meaning for us Jews:

> *And today's Muslims*
> *Revive Christendom's legacy*
> *Not only in the shabby,*
> *Now almost Jew-less*
> *Domain of Islam*
> *But in Islam's sullen diaspora*
> *On the continent of death*
> *Evil's favored home*
> *Where yesterday's Sieg Heils*
> *now sound as Allahhu akbar*

Today, indeed, the most active anti-Semitism in Europe does not come from nostalgic Nazis and agitated skinheads: it comes from members of "Islam's sullen diaspora", who are the perpetrators of a majority of the attacks on Jews and Jewish institutions in western Europe. The French government, in particular, does little to punish or deter attacks on Jews, preferring, it would appear, to appease the perpetrators than to protect their victims. And this is why, as I'm told, more and more Jews have emigrated from France in the past couple of years - they're just not up for another surge of Jew hatred on "the continent of death".

Here in Berlin I cannot help wonder what Islam's rapidly expanding penetration of the West will lead to; though it seems clear to me that it must indeed "lead to" something, for it is inherently de-stabilizing. In theory there would seem to be three broad possibilities. One is that the Muslims integrate with the Europeans; the second is that the Europeans integrate with the Muslims; and the third is that the Europeans remove the presence of Islam from their midst. But the first two of these do not, in fact, seem at all possible: for the Muslims will not give up Islam, and the Europeans will not embrace it. Nor do I believe that the Muslims will voluntarily depart from Europe or be satisfied with the relatively small portion of it that is already in their possession. Islamic dogma has it that every inch of this globe is either *dar-ul-islam* (the home of Islam) or *dar-ul-harb* (the home of the sword), and that it is incumbent upon the faithful to transform the one into the other - by the sword, if that's what it takes. On our part, here in the feeble West, we see this stark reality but we do not wish to acknowledge it. Islam we declare is a religion of peace; and we often refer to "the clash of civilizations" only to deny that it is occurring.

For the time being the people of the Muslim world show far greater fortitude in pursuing, than we in foiling, their dream of the global *dar-ul-islam*. But they can pursue it only up to the point where we resolve not to let them continue, for we are far stronger than they. When will we show this resolve? Prudence dictates that we should force the point sooner rather than later; folly, that we do so later rather than sooner. And since we no longer read our Thucydides and Hobbes and Machiavelli, I dare say that folly will win out. In fact, it is already doing so here in Europe. The Europeans are letting the pressure of Islam's presence in their midst grow to the point where they will soon no longer wish to endure it - and the horrific violence with which they will ultimately respond to it will not only have been forced upon them by the Muslims' expansionism, but by their own irresolution in containing this challenge during the time when relatively moderate action could still have been effective. One shouldn't forget that Europe is indeed *dar-ul-harb*, and not only in the sense intended by the Muslims. The Europeans have bloodletting - in their blood:

> *For Srebenica is an overture merely,*
> *pianissimo,*
> *To the grand chorale of Death,*
> *Which, perhaps not all that long, now,*

Will again sound its sublime chords
In a Europe of thunder and lightning.
And only the good people,
The people too good to do
What History requires
Will refrain from applause,
And they will be silent.

More on the *Gedenkbuch*. It has 75 names on each one of its 1838 pages – each line a murdered person, and then only from Germany! 1650 pages include place and date of death – good record keeping – the other 188 pages give the names of Jews whose place and date of death are unknown (*"ungeklaert"*). Among the latter I found a Moses Selzer (the same name as my grandfather's) who was born in 1893 and lived in Cologne. Until he stopped living, of course.

The three huge tomes were on the top of the checkout counter, for all to see; and unlike almost every other book in the library they were very well thumbed. I wonder how visibly the same books are placed in non-Jewish libraries in Germany – and how well-thumbed they are.

I couldn't deal with all those names; they blurred and disappeared; but I was stunned by their quantity. I would prefer a *Gedenkbuch* listing the names and biographical details of all those who participated directly or indirectly in the slaughter. Of all the murderers. Chances are good that it would contain very many more names than the Jewish volumes.

One of the best known and most tragic images of the Holocaust is the photograph of a German soldier aiming his rifle at a woman just a few paces from him who is shielding her small child and trying to flee.

I think that what we really notice in this photograph is the German soldier: and this, not so much because the image of him happens to be clearer than the image of the fleeing mother but because of the absolutely incomprehensible nature of what he is doing. There is, after all, nothing baffling about a mother fleeing from danger and trying to protect her child. That is a normal, predictable reaction to the situation. But the soldier – perhaps I should point out that he is an ordinary soldier, by German standards, and not an SS man – it is impossible to believe the evidence of one's eyes, which tell us with total certainty that here is a man aiming a loaded rifle at a defenseless woman who is clutching her small child to her breast, and that an instant after the photograph was taken this man will have pulled the trigger and, perhaps with just one shot, ended the lives of the mother and her child. We are astounded, outraged, profoundly dispirited by what this unspeakably evil man is going: but the important point to note here is that it is *him* whom we find riveting, and not the other.

And so it is, I think, with the entire genocide. We pity the victims. To some extent, we can identify with them even if we cannot imagine the terror they must have felt. Their anxiety, humiliation, despair, pain – in the last resort, we do all know something about suffering, even if not to the degree suggested by the photograph, and we fancy that we know something about death; certainly, death is a subject we can talk about. And so we can relate in a limited measure to what the woman in the photograph is experiencing, even though we cannot see her face and have no sense of who she is. Beyond that she and her child are little more than two of six million blurred shadows.

But what of the German? There is an absolute divide between him and anything we can imagine or can have experienced. What we see him do is absolutely beyond our ken, yet we see him with appalled clarity, and the horror and disbelief are imprinted indelibly in our souls.

It is he, not the woman and child, whom it is impossible for us to forget. For the six million shadows we feel whatever compassion one can feel for shadows. But the disgust, horror, anger we feel for this man are anything but shadowy, and they merge themselves into a feeling that entirely unambiguous. This is not a man – and his fellows are not men and women – about whom there is any uncertainty; we see who they are with excruciating clarity. We cannot avoid the sight of them. We cannot be indifferent to them. We cannot excuse or forgive them. What we can do, what I think we cannot avoid doing if we require of ourselves really to recognize what they did, is to feel and preserve unalloyed hatred for them and their kind.

There is an inscription on the back of this photograph recording that it was taken in the Ukraine on such and such a date; and we know that it was mailed home to someone in Germany. Now we are even more riveted by the horror we feel for this bestial man: evidently, he has friends, or family, or children in the *Heimatland*,

and he believes that they will be grateful for the evidence that the photograph provides them of how assiduously he and his comrades at the front are working to further the Fuehrer's mission and to further the interests of Germany. And the astonishment we feel at this almost makes us forget the tragedy that is about to befall a Jewish mother and child in the Ukraine.

How much more so, then, do we remember the murderers and not their victims when we read (in Goldhagen) that it was not all that uncommon for wives and girlfriends to visit their men at the front and watch them going about their work of shooting and bludgeoning Jews to death. Imagine this picture: Graetchen in her pretty *dirndl* clapping her hands in delight and jumping up and down excitedly as her Siegfried shoots a little Jewish child at more or less point blank range, fragments of its brains and bone actually spattering the hero's smart uniform! Truly, in this picture how much of our attention is on the child, and how much on the Germans? What memory do we carry away with us? That of yet another murdered child? Or that of the good German who murdered it and the glee of his woman as she watched him commit the crime? And which of the emotions we feel is the stronger and more durable? Our despair at the murder of the poor little child? Or our hatred of Siegfried and his Graetchen?

What immunizes me to Germans' judgment of Jews and empowers me to judge *them*? My hatred of them...

Another indication of how ineradicable Germany's past is was brought home to me when I noticed that today's Germans are apparently unsure of what to call their parliament. In some maps, brochures, and signs it is called the Bundestag, which is appropriate since it is the legislature of the Bund, or federation. But in others, and just as frequently, it is referred to as the Reichstag, (remember the Third Reich? Remember the Reichstag fire?), and occasionally as the Reichstag/Bundestag! It's as if they don't really want to let go of the Reich and all that it represents.

The hesitation I feel – to the not very considerable extent that I do, in fact, feel it – arises from the fantastic, incomprehensible, and almost unbelievable nature of what the Germans did when they were Nazis. It is so easy to feel, spontaneously, that none of this could ever have happened: to doubt whether my life (which has been so privileged, in many ways) really was in important measure shaped by the Nazis' doings. My doubt is not about the reliability of my knowledge, of course. It reflects my unfading shock and astonishment that the horrors occurred.

To be sure, I'm also trying to persuade myself that I am justified in regarding all Germans (but for the 410 "Righteous" among them) as belonging to *das Volk der Taeters* – the nation that did it. Strange, but I don't believe that I've ever met or heard of a German who asserts - or by his discomfort implicitly reveals - that he or she wasn't the other half of the Holocaust equation, that all this had nothing to do with him. So perhaps it is only outside Germany that we find people who are reluctant to regard all Germans as belonging to the doers' nation.

And for how long? For how many generations shall the sins of the fathers be visited upon the sons? Assume - so I can make the point I want to - that there is an infallible test to determine whether or not a particular German, we'll call him Adolf, (why shouldn't we?) is un-tinctured by even the slightest shade of anti-Semitism. This absolutely not anti-Semitic Adolf, who in fact hasn't yet been born, and won't be born for at least another two or three generations if ever: do I think that *he* belongs to *das Volk der Taeters* – to the people who did it?

The answer is: yes, I do think so. The Germans have scarred us terribly - those of us, that is, whom they did not actually kill. They have shown us that as Jews we are not safe from the most appalling cruelty, that we are not safe from murder, that there is nothing, not anything, that we can do to protect our children and other people we love. The Germans have shown us how *tentative* the Jew's existence really is, how tenuous our rights are, how seemingly indissoluble our links are to our ancient heritage as victims, how indifferent (at best) most people are to our fate. I know that in the 20th century other Jews were debased and even murdered by non-Germans, notably in Poland and Russia. But it seemed reasonable to believe that the pogroms and Slavic vileness belonged to the past, was merely the tail-end of "old Europe's" barbarism. *Incipit vita nova*, we thought. A new era has dawned, and all that horror is not going to be part of it, except as a rapidly-dimming memory. But the Germans showed us, in no uncertain way, how utterly wrong we were about this. They showed us that *all of that* can take place in the modern world just as it did in earlier eras. In fact, that it can occur even more devastatingly.

This knowledge is the birthright of every Jew - and people shouldn't fool themselves: just one Jewish grandparent can be enough to put you in that cattle car rolling slowly to a death camp. I have that knowledge, and it will remain with me as long as I live. Worse, far, far worse, my children too have that knowledge, and they will always be scarred by it. They may or may not feel particularly "Jewish". Perhaps they will marry Gentiles rather than Jews; perhaps they will not cultivate a knowledge of Jewish history, of the Hebrew language, of the Bible. But however they live their lives and even if they make no effort to make their Jewish heritage part of their lives, they will always know that they are Jews. And that means – this holds true of even the most marginal Jew, of the "not-non-Jew" - that they will always carry with them the knowledge of what can happen to them as Jews. They will carry the same scarring knowledge as I.

And for this reason it is both self-evident and completely proper that the Germans are to be hated, are to bear that mark of Cain that fits them so well - are to be scarred, in other words, for exactly as long as there are Jews who carry the scars that the Germans have incised into us. When there are no longer Jews who are haunted by the knowledge of what the Germans did to us, are no longer haunted by the entirely accurate knowledge that *all of that* can happen to them, too: only then (it seems to me) can a generation of Germans be born that does not deserve our hatred.

As long as we have to live with this terrible truth, the Germans must do so, too. Why should they not?

I noticed today that the people behind the reception desk at the hotel, who always struck me as cold and surly, are quite charming to other guests. Perhaps they are merely responding to my rather obvious hostility.

Thank goodness that tomorrow is my last day here. I've had passing fantasies about being confined here for the rest of my life, and the thought of leaving Berlin is almost too good to be true. This has been an ordeal. I don't feel as though I'm visiting a place I happen not to like, or that I'm a tourist who made a poorly-informed decision, or anything like that. I feel that I'm in a place that is fundamentally different from any I've ever been in before, a place that is dark and menacing, a place estranged by its own evil from the rest of humanity. It's only a little melodramatic to say that I've been on a pilgrimage to a temple of evil. Why pilgrimage? Why evil? Because I thought at first that I was here to acquaint myself with the victims, to see real people in the shadows into which those six million Jews were dissolved, and to feel at least some little part of their agony; but I discovered that the evil has overwhelmed them so completely that the shadows into which they were sent are almost totally impenetrable. In turn, I have learned that I can and must see those who caused this suffering, and that the final (I hope) irony is that the Holocaust is more about them, the Germans, than it is about the Jews. But where does that leave us, their victims? Only as the living, hating, rememberers.

Day Six

I'm out of Berlin – albeit in Munich, a town whose associations are hardly less charged than those of Berlin. Not for the first time, I'm struck by the confusion that seems to characterize so many German undertakings. The woman at the Lufthansa desk said that it would have been the easiest thing to get me out of Berlin on an earlier flight and at no extra charge – something that three long and expensive phone calls had led me to believe was impossible. And going from the terminal at which I'd arrived here to the one from which I will depart was like nothing so much as an outtake from a Marx Brothers movie. Just imagine what the Germans would have accomplished if they were as efficient as we think they are! On this trip I have found myself with a disturbing feeling that the world in which I functioned reasonably well and in which I was reasonably comfortable is moving away from me. It's as if I'm on a deserted station platform and the train that brought me here is pulling out of the station, leaving me standing with all the baggage of irrevocable decisions I have made during the course of my life.

Surely, this feeling reflects certain objective facts about myself: I am about to be 65 years old, after all. My children are already acting as though they need – so far, only occasionally! – to take care of me. But in Germany I really am a thing of the past; and seeing those sad old Russian Jews in the Berlin community center has only made that all the more obvious. Yet it is not only me. The Jews themselves, the entire Jewish people, seem also to be standing with their baggage on a deserted railway platform. It's not just the demography that I'm thinking of – though one can't exclude that, for Jewish fertility is well below replacement rates and intermarriage with non-Jews accelerates the decline at an enormous pace. It's also, and far more intractably, that we have not been very successful in defining what Jewish existence is to be in a world in which you have to be far more irrational than ever before in history to allow yourself to be defined by the messages that you would like to think God is beaming uniquely to you and your kind. We could see ourselves as a people who have been hated by more nations than any other in history, and who have survived a uniquely lengthy series of assaults. But I don't know where such a concept could take us. I rather suspect that in all our diversity and vagueness we are nowadays little more than a hated has-been people. I don't suppose that there's much of a future for a nation like that. Strange how I've come full circle. In my first book, which I wrote when I was 25, I dwelt at length, and ponderously, on the notion that all we can say of ourselves (that is, of everyone who can be called a Jew) is that we are not non-Jews. It's a logical progression, I suppose, from that definition (if that's what it is) to my current one that we are little more than a hated has-been-people, the "little more" having to do with such things as physical appearance (which many Jews don't in fact have) and knowledge of Jewish history, religion, ritual and the like (which ever-fewer Jews have). One is tempted to think of Israel as the exception to – the disproof of – all this. But Israel has its own dilemmas. The secular part of Israeli society, with which I identify, suffers from the same infertility as Jews in the West; and the same perplexity about what being Jewish is. The religious part of Israeli society, which I admire, are the fundamentalists who have all the answers. And these people are the true repository of Jewish values and purpose, and it may well be they and they alone who - in as little as two or three generations - will be the only ones left who actively consider themselves Jews:

> *And our children,*
> *One-half, one-quarter, one-eighth*
> *Of who we are,*
> *Not remembering what they never knew*
> *Will have no need to forget;*
> *And they will be at peace,*
> *Blithely descanting by Babylon's waters.*

Printed in Great Britain
by Amazon.co.uk, Ltd.,
Marston Gate.